THE GIFT OF PURPOSE

Unwrapping Your Unique Assignment

Brenda Mouzon, Ph.D.

authorHOUSE

AuthorHouse™
1663 Liberty Drive
Bloomington, IN 47403
www.authorhouse.com
Phone: 833-262-8899

Published by AuthorHouse 07/06/2023

ISBN: 978-1-6655-7972-8 (sc)
ISBN: 978-1-6655-7971-1 (e)

To my daughter, Moriah G. Mouzon

May you seek God's ways and never forget that you were born to follow Jesus, to serve Him faithfully, and to love others. May God use you and help unwrap His special assignment for your life.

TABLE OF CONTENTS

INTRODUCTION

The room was filled and hushed with excitement as all the little girls gathered around their teacher, Mrs. Johnson. She had promised them that today would be something special, and they were eager to find out what it was.

Mrs. Johnson smiled brightly at her students as she spoke in a gentle yet excited voice. "Girls, today is an extra-special day because we will learn about God's gift to us—our purpose!"

At this, the young ladies gasped in amazement and started asking questions, such as, "What is my purpose? How do I find it? What does it look like?"

Mrs. Johnson held up her hand for silence before continuing with the lesson plan for the day. She explained that just like unwrapping a gift or discovering something new, finding your purpose can be exciting. While it can be intimidating, if we trust in God's plans and stay focused on Him, He will reveal His perfect plan for our lives.

By now, each girl was sitting up straight in anticipation, ready to get started on her journey toward discovering her unique God-given gifts that were specifically tailored just for her. They talked among themselves about how amazing it would feel when they found out what their callings from God entailed, and they dreamed of becoming teachers, doctors, or even missionaries, depending on which paths God chose for them. It almost felt like Christmas morning when unwrapping presents under the tree—so much potential joy inside those packages just waiting to be discovered, if only they could wrap their fingers around them.

As Mrs. Johnson ended class, she reminded everyone not to forget that although seeking after their purpose can sometimes feel overwhelming, ultimately trusting in God's guidance throughout the process will ensure success, regardless of any outcome. As they left class that day, everyone felt inspired by her words and more hopeful than ever before.

Like Mrs. Johnson's girls, from the time we are born, we look forward to unwrapping our unique assignments from God— our purpose. We want to know why we're here and what we're supposed to do with our lives. Unfortunately, many of us never find that sense of purpose. We go through the motions, day after day, going to a job we hate, living for the weekends, and counting down the days until retirement.

But what if there's more to life than that?

What if we were put on this earth for a reason greater than our present positions?

It occasionally can be challenging for us to understand our purpose. So many voices shout at us and offer all kinds of distractions. The good news is that God doesn't ask us to accomplish a thousand or even a hundred things, so His Word majestically rises above the noise.

He merely requests that we concentrate on a few key factors that will enable us to accomplish His desire for those who love Him, to serve others, and to fulfill our purpose on earth and represent Him to the world. These are the fundamentals on His list on which we should concentrate our time and efforts, per Titus 2:3–5:

- Act in a godly manner.
- Speak honestly and respectfully.
- Exercise self-control and discipline.
- Be devoted to your husband.

- Be devoted to your children.
- Exercise discretion, and be wise in your actions.
- Be pure and modest, both within and out.
- Pay attention to your home.
- Be good and kind to everyone.
- Act as a mentor and motivator of virtue.

Knowing your life's purpose is incredibly liberating. It's also not as mysterious as you might imagine, based on this list. It is exhausting, irritating, and unsatisfying to float aimlessly through precious days, not knowing what you should do with yourself that would bring glory to God, blessings to others, and purpose to you.

These qualities might be present already in your life, and you might sense God directing you to use them in other ways. You might need to take some time to study Jesus's life; pay special attention to how He lived out God's purpose on a daily basis in the Gospels and how He kept His attention centered on God's purpose for Him.

Take heart. You already have a purpose, as you are a woman reading this right now. As you follow Jesus's directive to "seek first the kingdom of God," you are reflecting Him (Matthew 6:33).

Keep Your Eyes Fixed on God's Provision

Daily worries frequently cause us to stray from a set purpose. But consider this: if God has given you a purpose, He will be faithful to give you the necessary resources to achieve it. According to Paul's words in Philippians 4:19, "And my God will meet all your needs according to the riches of his glory in Christ Jesus." If you accept Jesus as your Savior, you and all other Christians will have all you need. You can always rely on God to provide whatever you need for sustenance.

Paul says God is faithful.

> No temptation has overtaken you except what is common to mankind. And God is faithful; he will not let you be tempted beyond what you can bear. But when you are tempted, he will also provide a way out so that you can endure it. (1 Corinthians 10:13)

The best part is that God has given us His unconditional blessing and the forgiveness of our sins through Jesus Christ. Therefore, those in Christ Jesus are no longer under condemnation (Romans 8:1).

God is faithful.

Allow this truth to renew your spirit. Because you overcome temptations, they strengthen your confidence in God; thus, He does not always eliminate them. He does, however, guarantee that the temptation won't get so intense that you can't resist it. Avoid attempting to handle your temptations by yourself. God gives you the ability to resist temptation through using prayer, the guidance of His Word, and the encouragement of others.

God has a plan for us, and when we align ourselves with His will, He will use us in ways we could never have imagined. Whether serving in our local churches, mentoring someone who is struggling, or simply being a friend to someone who needs one, we can all make a difference in the world. When we live on purpose, our lives have meaning. We are no longer drifting through life; instead, we are following God's plan for our lives.

As women, we are each uniquely designed by God with a particular purpose. Unfortunately, the world tells us that our value lies in our looks, possessions, and accomplishments. But the truth is that our worth comes from God alone. When we understand and embrace our true identities in Christ, we can live out His unique purpose for our lives.

This book will guide and encourage you as you seek to discover God's purpose for your life. Each chapter covers a different aspect of the journey, from defining your purpose to hearing God's voice and moving forward in faith. You will find practical advice, biblical insights, and personal stories to inspire you as you pursue the unique assignment God has prepared for you.

Whether you are just starting on the journey or have been searching for a while, this book will help you take the next step in unwrapping your *gift of purpose* with confident.

CHAPTER 1

THE FOUNDATION OF PURPOSE

> Therefore everyone who hears these words of mine and
> puts them into practice is like a wise man who built his
> house on the rock. The rain came down, the streams
> rose, and the winds blew and beat against that house;
> yet it did not fall, because it had its foundation on the
> rock. But everyone who hears these words of mine and
> does not put them into practice is like a foolish man
> who built his house on sand. The rain came down,
> the streams rose, and the winds blew and beat against
> that house, and it fell with a great crash." When Jesus
> had finished saying these things, the crowds were
> amazed at his teaching, because he taught as one who
> had authority, and not as their teachers of the law.
> (Matthew 7:24–29)

$\mathcal{F}$inding purpose brings us a deep sense of satisfaction and joy
as we are empowered to pursue the amazing plans that God has
for us. We can discover how our gifts, passions, and experiences
fit in with His divine plan through prayer and reflection. Being in
tune with the voice of God helps guide our steps on this spiritual
journey.

In Matthew 7:24–29, Jesus reminds us of the importance

of preparing for this spiritual journey. He encourages us to be as wise builders who build their houses on solid foundations to remain standing, even when storms come. Similarly, when we are aligned with God's will, it brings clarity and focus to our lives. Our purpose in life is found through a deep relationship with Him—understanding how He works in us and through us. We can see the blessings of alignment as we look back over our lives, grateful that He has guided us on our paths and has given us direction when needed.

Through prayer and obedience, we experience the fullness of what it means to be rooted in God. We gain strength for each step forward from knowing His presence within us, giving us courage no matter the circumstances. As we surrender to His will, our faith grows stronger, and we become more like Him.

The gift of purpose consists of being and acting in the ways that God wants for us to accomplish what He asks of us in our families, churches, and communities; becoming more like Christ; and then carrying out the unique assignment He has for each of us to undertake before we are laid to rest.

The gift of purpose is a deep privilege for all believers—an honor and joy to explore, discover, and fulfill. All too often in our human journey, we become overwhelmed by the world's distractions, temptations, and demands. Renewing our focus on Christ brings us back to our true identities and helps open up the possibilities that were always intended as part of our divine destinies. As we embrace His will for us as individuals within our families, churches, and communities—seeking to become more like Him in spirit—we can gain clarity concerning that unique calling He has planned just for us. Our reward? Confidence and joy in carrying out His special mission until it is complete!

To fulfill our purpose, however, we must heed Jesus's words in Matthew 7, where He gives a warning and an affirmation and hope—a caution to those who might disregard Jesus's message and a word of affirmation, hope, and encouragement to those who embrace it.

Thus, our God-given purpose is found in our strong relationship with God, a relationship built on Christ, the solid foundation. When we know Him and follow His leading, we will find our places in His plan. Our purpose is not just to exist but to live lives that glorify Him. We were created for His good works (Ephesians 2:10), and we can achieve them through obedience to Him (Matthew 7:24–29).

Often, however, we get caught up in the busyness of life and forget what truly matters. We can get so wrapped up in our plans and goals that we lose sight of God's bigger picture. When we keep Him at the center of our lives, everything else will fall into place.

In the years I have been walking with God and searching for my purpose in Him, I have learned that a woman's God-given purpose is based on three foundations: Christ, community, and calling.

Purpose in Christ

When I was younger, I often felt like I was searching for something without knowing what it was. I would get restless and antsy, feeling like there must be more to life than what I was experiencing. It wasn't until I found Christ that I realized what that "something" was. Christ gave my life purpose and meaning. He showed me that I was created for a specific reason and that my life had value. It took me years, however, to fully understand His purpose for my life (and I am still learning).

There's no possible way of discussing the foundation of purpose without first discussing our purpose in Christ Jesus.

Recently, a dear Christian woman told me, "I am learning what the purpose of my life is by taking a course on the subject." She was finishing an eight-week course that aimed to help people discover their calling. She told me that everyone in her class was eager to discover their purpose.

I heard a pastor on the radio advertise something similar. He offered to help listeners discover their spiritual gifts. If you asked him for the questionnaire, filled it out, and returned it to him, his staff would evaluate your particular gifts. Then they would tell you how to find your place in the body of Christ.

A very frustrated sister in the ministry wrote to me, "I have tried to find out how to fulfill God's will for my life. But I have found all sorts of hindrances. I have been so discouraged; at times I felt like giving up everything."

Perhaps this sister will turn to the sources that others are using. I am sure such tools are useful in one way or another, and I have used them. But the Bible says that God gives gifts to His children, and I believe there are unique callings for each of His children.

I am also convinced through scripture, however, that there is only one purpose for all believers. Our calling is inherent in a single purpose; every gift is born from this. And if we miss this purpose, all our desires and accomplishments will be in vain.

Jesus sums up this one purpose of ours in John 15:15:

> It is not you who have chosen me, but I have chosen you, and I have appointed you to go and bear fruit.

Our purpose is simply this: we have all been called and chosen to bear fruit.

What Is the Fruit That We Must Bear?

Many sincere Christians think that bearing fruit simply means bringing souls to Christ. But bearing fruit means more than just winning souls. The fruit that Jesus is talking about is the likeness to Him. In other words, bearing fruit means reflecting the likeness of Jesus. And the phrase "much fruit" means "an ever-greater likeness to Christ."

Growing more and more in the likeness of Jesus is our

primary purpose in life. It must be central to all our activities and our lifestyles and in our relationships. Indeed, all our gifts and callings—our work, ministry, and testimony—flow from this one purpose.

If I am not like Christ in heart—if I don't become more and more like Him—I have totally missed God's purpose for my life. It doesn't matter what I'm accomplishing for His kingdom; if I miss this purpose, I have lived, taught, and labored in vain.

God's purpose for me cannot be fulfilled with what I do for Christ. It cannot be measured by what I do, not even if I heal the sick or cast out demons. No, God's purpose is fulfilled in me only based on what I become in Him. The likeness to Christ is not what I do for the Lord but how I am transformed into His image.

The disciples of Jesus were pleased by their accomplishments, but Jesus gave His response contrary to their mindset. "Do you see all these great buildings?" replied Jesus. "Not one stone here will be left on another; every one will be thrown down." (Mark 13:2). Everything that is impressing you now—everything that appears so religious today—will be rejected. And it will happen because it does not reveal Christ. It is all centered on humans, not God.

The fact is that the disciples focused on the wrong temple. They had their eyes set on this man-made structure. Their gaze was on religious activity, and they had been impressed by the wrong things. What happened there did not represent the Father. The temple had become a den of robbers and money-changers.

In short, Jesus refocused the attention of the disciples on the spiritual temple, as Paul would later write to the church: "Do you not know that your body is the temple of the Lord?" (1 Corinthians 6:19). Like the disciples, many of us are impressed by the large church buildings, by the multitudes that flock there on Saturdays and Sundays, by the peculiarity of the worship services, by the many programs, and by the many ministries. But Jesus's message is clear: we should not focus on buildings made of stone and metal, on forms of worship, or on impressive sermons.

On the contrary, our gaze should be on our spiritual temple that houses the Holy Spirit.

The Holy Spirit desires to live in our hearts. And He is always ready to fulfill His purpose in us. This means that we must have our spiritual homes in order.

Jesus was totally dedicated to the Father, which was enough for Him. In fact, He said, "I do not do or say anything except what my Father tells me" (John 12:49; John 5:19–20). Likewise, every believer must follow the same model.

Do you want to bear "much fruit" that comes from the likeness of Christ?

I asked myself this question as I prepared to write this book. And the Spirit whispered to me, "You must be willing to look at yourself in the light of Jesus Christ and the Father's will for your life."

To put it simply, bearing fruit comes from how we treat people. We fulfill our purpose in life when we begin to love others as Christ loves us. And we grow more and more in the likeness of Christ as our love for others grows. Jesus said, "As the Father loved me, so I loved you: continue in my love" (John 15: 9). His commandment is clear and simple: "Go and love others. Give to others the unconditional love that I have given to you."

The Spirit pointed out to me three areas where bearing fruit allows us to unwrap God's gift of purpose in our lives:

1. We understand our true identities in Christ.

As much as I want to "go and love others," I must have a sense of who I am in Christ to truly share His love with others. When I receive my gift, I have to not only unwrap it but also use it to learn what He says about me and my identity in Him. I've learned that our purpose is wrapped up in the gift of grace that God has placed within us. It is our job to unwrap it and see what He has in store for our lives. Knowing who we are in Christ, understanding

His truth, and letting it soak into our hearts will help us to bear real fruit—not just any kind of fruit but a sweet and lasting fruit that makes an eternal impact on our lives and in the lives of those around us. By deepening our relationships with God, our true identities emerge from the depths of His love that resides within us. We accept it, believing and trusting that His plan for us will be full of joy, grace, forgiveness, compassion, and, ultimately, a richness of bearing much fruit for His kingdom!

To bear fruit from your purpose and find true identity in Christ, you must unwrap the gift of who He has made you to be. Identifying your talents, strengths, and possibilities for growth can open the door to using your God-given resources for kingdom pursuits.

Consider taking time alone with God and His Word, reflect on His promises, and uncover the depths of who He is calling you to be. True identity in Him will come only when you view yourself through His lens and understand that bearing good fruits that honor His name pleases Him deeply. Take courage in knowing you have all that you need within you already to fulfill this call, so get out from under the covers and start living an unwrapped life.

Here is how it works:

In Colossians 3:4, Paul states that when we put on the new self and remember our true identities in Christ, "We will bear fruit in every good work." In other words, our gifts of purpose serve a very real purpose—to bring about spiritual growth. When we unwrap these gifts, carefully studying them and the implications for our lives, this eventually leads us to understand who we are in Christ. Then, by taking action based on what He reveals to us through this gift, we will undoubtedly bear more fruit than if we chose not to unwrap it. We have been given a fantastic purpose; let's use it to love and serve others, including families and those not within our circle.

2. We bear fruit by unwrapping our gifts of purpose to love and serve our families.

Jesus's words in the Gospels are encouraging and remind us of His immense love for each of us. We often forget that Jesus wants us to extend the same love He has for us to those closest to us. This means I will show my husband, children, and other family members the unconditional love that Jesus shows me. It means striving to be intentional in my words when talking to them. It also means making an effort to speak positive affirmations in their lives daily by supporting them, both verbally and nonverbally.

Bearing fruit in my home looks like spending quality time with my family, even in a world filled with various distractions. This means carving out intentional moments with each family member, whether going on a hike together, saying a night prayer as a unit, or even little things like asking how their day went.

Giving time to our family members through attendance and focus helps them feel seen and valued as individuals in our households. The definition of love is putting another person's needs first. With thoughtfulness and care for others centered around God's love for us, our gift of purpose can permit us to do just that in our homes.

Bearing the fruit of my gift of purpose also means teaching my children to adopt virtues like gratitude, respect, and integrity, in addition to my acting as a peacemaker in the family. I can show appreciation for their contributions inside and outside the home by praising them when they do something right or correcting them gently when they make a mistake. I also can help my husband develop his sense of purpose by encouraging him during his highs and lows. Loving someone is more than just expressing it through words; it's about showing it through compassion and understanding. By using my gift of purpose with intentionality and humility, I will show how much love I have for my husband and children every single day

But the struggle is real.

It can be challenging to always express this kind of love, especially when we don't feel loved in return, but by doing so, we can bear the excellent fruit that Jesus refers to in His statement in John 15:15. When I look at those closest to me—my husband and children—it's easy to recognize that the best way to show them my love is to extend unconditional kindness and acceptance.

My faith in Jesus Christ drives this love, which gives me the courage and power to extend it even when others may not deserve it. To bear fruit in His name means that I know that by loving those around me, I can build a legacy unchanged by time or circumstance.

Loving the people in our homes is one way we can live out God's promise and share the spirit of God!

3. We bear the fruit of our gifts of purpose by how we treat those who are not close to us.

The Bible calls us to show love and kindness to those with whom we do not have a close relationship—the people we encounter daily and humankind as a whole. I'm learning that this takes effort. It looks like giving out genuine compliments or taking an extra minute to talk to someone who may feel lonely. These small acts of kindness can significantly impact someone's day and bring joy into my life.

Bearing fruit through my gift of purpose looks like my offering words of encouragement to those around me, whether they are relatives, neighbors, friends, colleagues, or anyone who seeks my help. By taking the time to offer a smile, look someone in the eye, or show genuine interest in someone, I'm expressing that I recognize the person's value and importance. I proactively seek more tangible forms of love, when appropriate and necessary. Whether it's helping someone with a project, praying for him or her, listening to someone's story, or offering practical support in any form, I am using my gift of purpose to demonstrate an outward display of love that brings light into the world, which radiates from both me and my fellow human being.

In my journey toward bearing fruit through my gift of purpose, I'm discovering the importance of living with intentionality—mindful of how my words and actions affect others. When I live with intentionality, my life reflects my faith, and my God-given gifts become evident in my actions. Living intentionally allows me to use the talents I have been given for the benefit of others, an act that brings joy and fulfillment to my life. Intentionality helps me focus on what matters most—living out my faith and sharing it with those around me.

As I take the time to pause and be mindful of my choices, decisions, thoughts, and feelings each day, my faith is strengthened, and my life begins to bear more fruit. With every step I take in this direction, I am reminded that although bearing fruit is hard work, I have a Father who cares about how I use my gifts to show His goodness to others.

It is God's will that we use these gifts to bear fruit that will draw those to God who do not know Him.

Ultimate Expression of Bearing Fruit
through the Gift of Purpose

I have learned that my purpose is founded in Christ. This means that, first and foremost, I must learn to love God with all my heart, mind, soul, and strength (Mark 12:30). From this foundation of loving God comes everything that He calls His daughters to do. We are called to love others (1 John 4:7), to serve His church (Galatians 5:13), and to boldly proclaim the gospel (Matthew 28:19–20).

We are also called to be wives and mothers and to build our homes on the foundation of Christ (Ephesians 5:22–33). In everything we do, our goal should be to glorify God and enjoy

Him forever (1 Corinthians 10:31). As we seek to fulfill our purpose in Christ, He will equip us with everything we need to accomplish His plan for our lives (Philippians 4:13).

We seek to honor Him and to make His name known in everything we do. We want to be a light for others, pointing them to the hope and life that is found in Christ. When we live our lives for Him, everything else falls into place. Our relationships, our careers, our hobbies—everything takes on new meaning when we view it through the lens of Christ.

How do you find your purpose in Christ?

Many of us already know that the foundation of our purpose is in Christ. Most often, we struggle with what that means and what that looks like.

If you have wondered how to find your purpose in Christ, here are a few clues that can help guide you on your journey:

1. Pray and ask God to reveal His plan for your life.
2. Study the Bible, and meditate on scripture.
3. Talk to wise, godly people who can give you godly counsel when you are making decisions about your life.
4. Get involved in serving opportunities in your church and community.
5. Use your gifts and talents to bless others.
6. Be flexible and open to what God may be leading you to do.
7. Don't fear stepping out in faith, and trust God with the outcome.

Purpose in Community

Christian women find purpose in the community. We were created for relationships, and it is in the community that we can best support and encourage one another. It can be intimidating to discover our purpose in God's grand cosmic scheme, but we're not meant to go it alone. Being part of a Christian community has numerous advantages, one of which is that it encourages us to find our callings and live out who God created us to be.

We were designed to interact with one another. With all of its challenges, this life is too much for us to handle alone. We yearn for community. In addition to our purposes, we can participate in the purpose of the entire body of believers. Communities can have a significant impact on the global community. Large corporations know this and frequently employ teams and groups for the best results. Success is inevitable when there is shared commitment and everyone works toward the same objective.

Collaboration among groups also results in the development of a culture that is later transferred to the surrounding environment. It can be done only by a group. An individual can have an impact on others, but he or she cannot alter a society on his or her own.

Our involvement in the Christian community is essential to God's larger plan for us. The amazing thing is that no matter where you are in God's plan, you can start serving and participating in your church and with other believers immediately. You eventually will discover that you are being steered and led in the right direction. As you look to God together and follow His direction, the individuals serving beside you will help you to find your purpose. I've learned that God guides in stages, but the people with whom you surround yourself will help you perceive these stages as God guides you.

As a result, it's crucial to be a part of a local Christian community that can aid in defining your identity. By ourselves, we are like a puzzle piece that is looking for its place outside of the puzzle box. We are designed to interact intricately in ways beyond our ability to comprehend or observe. God is aware of our collaborative efforts. He wants to use us because He sees the broader picture. We must be near the other pieces to determine our place in the puzzle.

God's calling on our lives is never truly complete, and it continually evolves. God demands more of us as our level of faith increases. He may ask us to work harder at what we are doing presently, or He may radically alter our goals and surroundings. No matter what, He always wants us to be members of a Christian community to support and nurture our growth. Community helps us discover our purpose, refine our purpose, and help us work together in our purpose.

Purpose of Calling

A Christian woman's purpose is also found in her calling. Each of us has been uniquely created and called by God to impact the world around us for His glory. Once we have discovered our purpose, how do we fulfill it faithfully and with excellence?

Knowing who we are in Christ gives us meaning. God has a specific purpose and a particular calling for every one of us. Our primary purpose is to follow Jesus as disciples. Our distinctive secondary callings result from our obedient responses to the primary calling.

When we attempt to compel all women into one limited vision of the role and responsibilities of women, the body of Christ loses out. Because of Christ's transformation, we are not required to follow other good and holy people's advice without question. We will never understand our genuine purpose in life if we are merely happy to get along for the sake of getting along. As we seek clarity on our spiritual journeys, a wonderful mentor and a secure community of Christians persistently will direct us to Christ and urge us to follow Him. A godly mentor calls us to entirely submit our wills and desires to God's will for our lives, while serving as examples of Christ's character.

All things were created by God, and His expansive, creative vision encompasses women from all origins, stages of life, and civilizations. His goals for His kingdom are timeless. Young women who dedicate themselves to prayer, like Rhoda, and virgins, like Mary, the young mother of Jesus, are included in His will. His intentions are expansive enough for women like Elizabeth, Rachel, and Hannah—all of whom endured protracted seasons of infertility. His intentions extend to rejected, bereaved, adulterous women, like the Samaritan lady at the well, and women with pagan pasts, like Ruth and Rahab. He observes ancient ladies, like the prophetess Anna, and downtrodden and enslaved women, like Hagar. Because all women are a part of God's purposes and plans, we lovingly embrace women like these. You are part of God's plan as well!

Sadly, our environment continuously sends women signals that say, "You are not valuable. You are not capable of earning that level of income. You are not educated enough for this position. To wear those jeans, you need to be thinner. You are not physically appealing enough to date that man or to get a man to truly commit to you. You are not qualified to hold a leadership position. You are a terrible parent. You are not a great wife."

It's simple to belittle or reject women who are either more self-assured than we are or who have made different decisions from our own when we feel uneasy or inadequate. Such a rejection somehow improves our self-esteem and makes us more confident in our decisions, if only momentarily.

Once you have found your purpose and have begun to live it out, what are some common challenges and obstacles you may face along the way? How can you discover your purpose and live by it?

Discovering Your God-Given Purpose

God always determines the purpose of a thing before He creates it. This is why even before He created you, He already knew the purpose for which He would create you.

God reveals two things when you meet Him: your identity in Christ and the purpose for which He created you. When you do not know the purpose of your life, sooner or later you will ask yourself the meaning of life: "Why am I on earth? What is the purpose of my existence?"

The Bible says,

> For in him all things were created: things in heaven and on earth, visible and invisible, whether thrones or powers or rulers or authorities; all things have been created through him and for him. (Colossians 1:16)

If you want to know why you were placed on earth, you must ask your Creator, God. You were born by Him and for Him. God always determines the purpose of a thing before creating it. This is why even before He created you, He already knew the purpose for which He would create you. Many people fail to find their life's purposes because they think from within themselves and ask themselves questions:

- What do I want to become?
- What will I do with my life?
- What are my goals?
- What are my projects, my desires, my passions?

We do not find the purpose of our existence by focusing on ourselves. By focusing on God, however, we arrive there.

God is not only the starting point of your life; He is the source.

To discover your life's purpose, you must turn to the manual of your creation—the Word of God, the Bible—and not to the world, its wisdom, and the sorts of alternative solutions it offers you. You can choose your profession, your spouse, your hobbies, and other aspects of your life but not your reason for being.

Here are some typical questions from a person who does not know the purpose of her life:

- Why was I created as a woman and not a man?
- Why was I born in this country?

- Why was I born into this family?
- Why am I alive?
- Why wasn't I born in another era?
- Why wasn't I born like this or like that?

These questions often reveal that you have not discovered your life's purpose as a woman. When you know your life's purpose, you don't devalue yourself because you know that your presence on earth is not an accident. You know you are not a mistake, a coincidence, or the result of two people meeting. You are aware of the role you have to play in your generation to advance the reign of God on earth. You exist because God had prepared, long before the foundation of the world, a precise plan for your life.

Remember this: God created you for a purpose. You were born to succeed, not to fail. You are destined to shine in your generation and reflect the glory of your God on earth, like Deborah, Ruth, and Esther.

> For he chose us in him before the creation of the world to be holy and blameless in his sight. In love he predestined us for adoption to sonship through Jesus Christ, in accordance with his pleasure and will— to the praise of his glorious grace, which he has freely given us in the One he loves. (Ephesians 1:4–6)

Likewise, followers of Jesus know that

> And we know that in all things God works for the good of those who love him, who have been called according to his purpose. For those God foreknew he also predestined to be conformed to the image of his Son, that he might be the firstborn among many brothers and sisters. And those he predestined, he also called; those he called, he also justified; those he justified, he also glorified. (Romans 8:28-30)

Therefore, it is up to us to put our lives at our Creator's service, release our potential, and play the role He has ordained for our lives.

The story is told of a girl who stood out. She was the kind of person who frequently was called an "old soul." While other children ran around the playground, chasing each other, she contemplated life's vast and profound mysteries. For as long as she could remember, she had pondered the meaning of life, sought knowledge, wondered if there was an afterlife, and yearned for "enlightenment." You might say that she had, since she was a young child, "eternity written on her heart" (Ecclesiastes 3:11). She was ignorant of God, but she firmly thought that we all have a specific mission to accomplish in this life. Back then, she would have referred to it as *fate*.

She was as eager as most people were to learn what her purpose was, but she never would have thought that it would take her thirty-five years to figure it out. Thank God that Jesus is a patient person.

I was that little girl.

Today, I am much more interested in hearing about your dreams and purposes than giving the intricacies of my own, which are God-given. My first concern while considering committing my life to God was losing control. *Sharing this new knowledge with others will be boring*, I thought, *a challenge, too grave, too perilous.* Let me tell you this, if you're wondering if that's the case today—it's *not* those things at all! I must argue that you are mistaken you think anything God has called you to is boring, overly controlling, or mundane. God cherishes you too much to call to a purpose that would not glorify Him and bring passion to your life. He genuinely has the most unique, rewarding activities for you to do. He wants to be near to you, to truly love you, to fix the parts of you that are damaged, and to guide you into a plan that will change the world after you leave it.

You will find your life in Him when you lay down your life (Matthew 10:39). The key is *trust*. It involves having faith that

He is looking out for your best interests, that He understands you better than you understand yourself, and that, in the end, you will realize it was totally worthwhile to surrender yourself to Him.

Why Are You Here and Who Are You?

I believe we frequently have it backward. God wants to start with *who we are* when we ask for guidance on what to do.

Do you already know? Has it seeped into your flesh, blood, and very being? You become a child of God if you accept Jesus as your Savior and want Him to rule over your life. You were created to serve His people, to be whole, to praise Him, and to live out His Word. Do you accept these claims? God frequently waits until you have a firm understanding of the *who* before revealing the *what* for your life.

Let's now explore the most effective methods of seeking God and learning your unique reason for existing in this place.

Five Keys to Understanding Why You're Here

1. Recognize the voice of God.

Do you realize that God will address you personally? When I first heard God's voice some years ago, His voice absolutely blew my mind. This, in my opinion, is one of the guiding principles of our spiritual journeys. Period. It's also outrageously cool.

Jesus says that if we accept Him as our Savior, we will be able to recognize His voice. Spend as much time as you can reading His Word to start hearing His voice. "My sheep listen to my voice; I know them, and they follow me." (Matthew 10:27)

Romans 10:17 states, "Faith comes by hearing, and hearing by the word of God."

Since God isn't the only one speaking, we must also learn to distinguish between the other voices. The voices of the world,

Satan, and our flesh are also present. Here's the problem: shouldn't we hear the directives directly from God if we wish to carry out what He would have us do with our lives?

This cannot be skipped. It must be on our lists of things to accomplish. When my time on earth is finished, I don't want to stand before God's throne and be told that I failed to fulfill the purpose for which He placed me on this planet. I hope and pray that you will put Him and His voice first.

We shall always stay on the winding road that leads to life by hearing and obeying, and it also always will be a great joy.

2. Expand your strengths and abilities.

This one caught me off guard a little bit because it appeared a little too temporal. But even so, focusing on my personal development and skill-building offered God much room to express the abilities He has given me. A mentor once said to me that God can more easily guide a moving vessel. I didn't hear anything from God while I was motionless and frozen. (Don't miss that at all.) For the love of God, there is a place and a time to simply be still, but there is also a place where we can step forth in faith with our hearts open to God and rely on Him to guide (or reroute) our paths. The key is to hold everything in our hands lightly because if we don't, it will ache when God pries our fingers open. Let's prioritize God and His will in our thoughts and actions.

3. Step aside for God.

I won't lie; I'm sure I still obstruct God occasionally. But generally speaking, to receive what He has for you, you must let go of what you had planned: You have to lay down your will, your way, your wants, your walk, your worship, and your warfare, your viewpoints, your religion, and your restrictive beliefs.

I don't claim it's simple, but it is essential. How will we make room for God's plans if we focus on our own? In my experience, when I'm holding on to myself too firmly, I can't even hear what He's speaking to me. To get the specifics of my purpose from Him, He had to open my mind to many things.

If you do this, enlist the aid of the Holy Spirit. Simply say in your prayer, "Lord, I'm willing to be made willing. I will be whatever you want me to be." Remain in His Word, in prayer, and in worship. It won't take long when you are soaking it in while in His presence. Once His goodness is revealed to you, it will be simple to let go of the past and give way to something entirely new (2 Corinthians 5:17).

4. *Keep seeking God until you truly understand who you are—and accept it.*

Before we started this list, I briefly touched on this. We are on a quest to learn two important facts about ourselves in this life: (1) who we are, and (2) why we are here, namely and personally. We need to be careful not to mix up the two.

You must first consider who God is to determine who you are. You may laugh at this, but you can hear and recognize His voice by spending time in His Word. Even if your life is a tempest, you will feel at peace once you *discover* who you are and *recognize* who you are. You will sense safety. Your viewpoint will be eternal. You will have a strong sense of faith. Your spiritual and natural gifts will be evident to you, although they still might need work. And you will be prepared to get your orders.

5. *Start your path to recovery and soul renewal.*

You know the saying, "She's got baggage," right? In reality, it applies to all of us. We use it to describe people we think are overly dramatic, problematic, or high maintenance, even those who seem to have it together and never show signs of becoming upset in public. We all have one or more heartbreaking events that are a part of our history because life is complicated. God knows better than to maintain a stiff upper lip, push discomfort to the side, and act indifferent. Abuse, desertion, and rejection hurt. The only way to heal from a wound is to move through the pain under the direction of the Holy Spirit and Jehovah Rapha, the Lord our healer. We may try to avoid it or get around it or take medication. If we don't, we carry baggage into the subsequent chapter of our existence. Without a doubt, we can carry out our objectives the best when we are entirely under His guidance. Furthermore, I think that once we are under the Holy Spirit's guidance, God can explain our purpose to us most clearly. And His voice appears to be clearer when our hearing is at its optimum.

CHAPTER 2

THE WOMAN OF PURPOSE

But I have raised you up for this very purpose, that I might show you my power and that my name might be proclaimed in all the earth. (Exodus 9:16)

She speaks with wisdom, and faithful instruction is on her tongue. (Proverbs 31:26)

*T*he dictionary definition of *woman* is "an adult female human being," while *purpose* is "our reason for being and for what we do." We are on earth for this reason. Each of us has a certain life purpose, and it is up to us to find that purpose and carry it out. We will benefit from and be a blessing to others by doing this. The Bible says,

> To everything there is a season and a time to every purpose under the heaven. (Ecclesiastes 3:1)

> And we know that for those who love God, to those who are called according to His purpose, all things work together for good. (Romans 8:28)

The Acts of the Apostles describes how God anointed Jesus of Nazareth with the Holy Ghost and with authority, and He went about doing good and healing everyone who was under the influence of the devil. Jesus recognized His purpose and that He was called to do good to others (Acts 10:38).

If you are a woman, you must ask yourself, "Why am I here? Why do I exist? What am I doing here? To whom have I been sent?" To lead a fulfilling life, you must figure out your life's purpose.

The Bible shows examples of women who found their callings and led fulfilled lives; I will talk about two of these women from the Bible: Deborah and Esther.

Esther's purpose was to strategically deliver the Jews. She found favor before the king when she made her request. Before her uncle Mordecai talked to her about the impending evil planned against the Jews, she had not accomplished much in her life. She was reminded that death hung in the air, which gave her the courage to step forth into the realm of preparation and prayer. She gave herself entirely to her purpose and was willing to die for her people. It was reported that she said, "If I perish, I perish." Esther realized that her purpose in the palace wasn't merely to indulge in the luxuries of life; she realized that preserving her people's lives was her ultimate purpose even if it meant the end of her life.

Take some time to reflect and ask yourself why you are currently on earth. Unless you understand why you are here, you will merely exist and not have a fulfilling life.

In the Book of Judges, Deborah served as a judge in Israel, a prophet, and a wife. She assisted the Israelites in defeating their adversaries. Deborah accompanied Barak to the front lines because he had promised to go without her. What has God commanded you to do, woman? He will grant you the grace to complete it, once you find it and concentrate on it.

In modern life, a woman who led an extraordinary life was Mother Teresa. She devoted her life to helping the sick and the less fortunate. Her organization founded a leper colony, a hospice, and facilities for the elderly, blind, and crippled. She won the Nobel Peace Prize in recognition of her humanitarian efforts.

I want you to know that finding your mission will give your life more clarity, concentration, and direction. You must find your purpose and become who God has created you to be if you want to live a meaningful life or change the world. Your skills, abilities, and gifts must be put to use for the good of others.

Finally, I want you to make up your mind today to be a woman of purpose. Be deliberate in all you do. Pray and reflect on the Bible. Let God speak to you because hearing from Him will help you achieve your goals. You will experience unimaginable fulfillment and blessings when you live according to God's plan, and your life will acquire significance and meaning.

Esther, The Woman of Purpose (Her Importance)

I can still clearly recall how young I was when I first heard the biblical story of Esther—the orphan who became a courageous queen and saved Israel from oblivion; the young woman who became queen after being taken to the king's palace; the one who bravely fought to protect her people from the cruel enemy plans. Yet as we dig deeper into this incredible story, there is so much more. Its ten chapters make evident some extremely potent truths, great wisdom for today, and the knowledge that God still acts mightily on behalf of His people (Esther 1–10).

Quick Facts about Esther

- Esther was taken from her home and brought to live in the palace along with numerous other harem girls. She was Jewish, but, as Mordecai had advised her, she never disclosed her nationality or family background. She received favor from God and quickly ascended to the throne.

- The Book of Esther is one of two books in the Bible that are named after women. Ruth being the other.
- Esther is one of only two books in the Bible that does not explicitly mention God by name (the other is Song of Songs). Although God's name is not mentioned in the narrative, His omnipotence and sacrificial love are evident in all the words and chapters.
- It takes place at a time when Jews faced intense racial hatred. They had long been an underrepresented group in Persia.

My desire to be a woman like Esther grew as I learned more about her life from the Bible. When I was young, hearing about Esther's bravery and loyalty inspired me to submit my life and future to God's plans.

Numerous publications discuss the significance of the Jewish orphan who became a Persian queen, historically and theologically. While many have noted Esther's impact on history, Esther had such a profound impact on my personal life that I feel compelled to tell it from my point of view. Why was Esther so significant? Who was she? The following insightful lessons are drawn from her story:

God Uses Ordinary People

At the time Esther was born, Israel was held captive as punishment for their disobedience to God. Esther was taken in by her cousin Mordecai after her parents were slaughtered. Esther was a typical woman living in a foreign country. She belonged to a lowly minority race, so much so that Mordecai counseled her to conceal her Jewish heritage when she ultimately was chosen to be queen (Esther 2:10).

God picked Esther to carry out His preconceived purposes through her.

When I first learned this fact as a little girl, I thought, *If God has a purpose to use an ordinary girl like Esther, maybe He has a purpose for my life too* (Ephesians 2:10).

Paul says,

> Now all these things happened to them as an example, but they were written for our instruction. (1 Corinthians 10:11)

Imagine if God wrote Esther's story to teach you and me not only from her example but also to demonstrate how He acts sovereignly in the lives of regular people who obediently follow His rules.

Esther did not allow her circumstances to make her bitter.

The suffering that young Esther experienced during her upbringing is beyond my comprehension. She would have been one of many Jewish youngsters who lost their parents during that turbulent time. The Bible claims that Esther was obedient to Mordecai while she was raised by him, refusing to rebel or feel resentment toward him (Esther 2:20).

Esther's heart was delicate and obviously sympathetic toward others. This is in contrast to those people who have grown up in difficult circumstances and who tend to doubt God's love; they develop a distrust of both God and others.

Esther was forced to participate in the king's beauty contest after she was seized. If she were to lose her virginity in the process, she would become the king's property and would never be permitted to return to her life with Mordecai, whether or not he picked her as his wife (Esther 2:14). With such little control over her past or future, another lady could have reacted negatively, but not Esther. She had faith in God.

Esther Was Not Prideful, despite Her Beauty

The second chapter of Esther attests to the fact that she was a stunning lady. She was granted access to twelve months of pampering and therapies to enhance her beauty, along with all the other exquisite virgins.

As the harem of virgins awaited their one night with the king, I can only imagine the cattiness that would have taken place. Esther's humble nature, however, shone through, and she gained the respect of everyone who saw her, including Hegai, the king's eunuch, who had been given custody of the virgins (Esther 2:15). When the king summoned a virgin, she was free to bring whatever she felt would appeal to the king the most. When Esther was called, she brought nothing but the advice Hegai had given, which got the king's attention.

God Had Absolute Control Over the King's Heart

God changed the king's heart, such that he "loved Esther more than all the ladies, and she won grace and favor in his sight" when she spent the night with him (Esther 2:17). Knowing that the king's heart was actually in the Lord's hands and that God turns it anywhere He pleases gives us hope (Proverbs 21:1). We can take comfort in the knowledge that God chooses leaders and uses them to carry out His purpose, whether they are godly leaders or not, even in these times, when politics seem to be our only chance.

Esther Desired Elder Mentors

We saw the intensity of Mordecai's devotion to his little cousin as he constantly strove to find out about her well-being as Esther awaited her night with the king. Just picture Mordecai's compassion for his beloved Esther. Mordecai revealed himself as

God-fearing man with a great sense of judgment, once Esther became queen. He revealed to Esther a murderous plot against the king that he had discovered, thus saving the king's life (Esther 2:21–21).

When Mordecai discovered a second plan to exterminate the Jews, he asked Esther to ask the king to intervene. Mordecai helped her to understand why God had chosen her to be queen when she initially denied out of fear. He warned,

> You and your father's house will perish if you remain mute at this time; help and deliverance will come to the Jews from another area. Who knows if you haven't arrived in the kingdom at this precise moment? (Esther 4:14)

According to Titus 2, God's intention has always been to guide the next generation in understanding and adhering to His ways. Wherever you are in life, follow Esther's lead and look to wiser, more godly mentors to lead you over the stormy waves, with your eyes fixed on Christ. Remember that someone younger than you always needs to learn from your experience. Take a lesson from Mordecai.

Courageous Was Not Her First Response to God's Call

Esther initially hesitates to take bold action. This reluctance, far from detracting from her heroine status, actually makes her more relatable and realistic. As a Christian woman, I appreciate Esther's initial reaction, which mirrors my own tendency towards caution when faced with challenging situations. It takes a lot of courage to step out of one's comfort zone and take risks, especially when the stakes are high. In Esther's case, the stakes were literally life and death, and she needed Mordecai's encouragement and prodding to take action. This is a reminder that even heroes and heroines need support and motivation to overcome their fears and doubts. As we navigate our own challenges and uncertainties, let us draw inspiration from Esther's bravery and the knowledge that we too can overcome our fears with faith and perseverance.

Esther—A Biblical Character Who Knew Where to Get Her Power

After hearing Mordecai's words of wisdom, Esther understood that her ascent to royalty had nothing to do with her physical beauty or that God had given her a comfortable life. Esther instinctively understood she needed to rely on God for strength.

> "Go, assemble all the Jews ... hold a fast on my behalf," she retorted. "The same will be done by me and my young women." (Esther 4:15–16)

Esther Awaited God's Appointed Time

Esther waited for the Lord's timing which played a crucial role in the eventual salvation of her people. Esther was faced with a daunting task - approaching the king to plead for the lives of her fellow Jews. But instead of jumping into action, Esther prioritized prayer and fasting, seeking God's guidance and wisdom.

Little did Esther know, God was already at work behind the scenes. The king was plagued by insomnia, and in his restlessness, he ordered the chronicles of his reign to be read to him. As he listened, the king was reminded of Mordecai's loyalty and heroism in saving the king's life. This prompted the king's admiration and respect for Mordecai, ultimately leading him to issue a decree allowing the Jews to defend themselves against their would-be attackers.

Oh, the beauty of God's perfect timing and orchestration! Even though Esther may have felt uncertain and anxious during her waiting period, the Lord was already working in ways she could not see. The story of Esther teaches us to remain vigilant and prayerful, trusting in the Lord's sovereignty and goodness even when we can't see the bigger picture.

As women of faith, let us take heart in Esther's example and allow God to guide us in our own waiting periods. Let us diligently seek His wisdom and trust in His timing, knowing that His plans for us are good and perfect, just as they were for Esther and her people.

Esther Valued Her Community More than Her Own Life

"If die, I die." (Esther 4:16)

When we reflect on Esther's story, it is clear that she was a remarkable woman who made a profound impact on her people. While we may never know the full extent of how her actions influenced the course of history, we can be certain that her bravery and unwavering faith played a vital role.

It is awe-inspiring to consider that Esther was able to prioritize her love for God and her people above her own desires and ambitions. By surrendering herself to His will, she was able to achieve something far greater than any individual accomplishment could ever provide. For Christians and women everywhere, Esther's example serves as a beacon of courage and inspiration.

When we contemplate the possibility of uttering these very same words, our hearts may race with fear and trepidation. We may wonder if we would have the strength of character to follow through with such a commitment, or if we would fall short of the mark. However, as Christians, we must remind ourselves that it is through God's grace and providence that we are able to accomplish anything at all.

If we are to walk in Esther's footsteps and embody her brand of bravery, we must first cultivate our faith in God and seek wisdom from those who have gone before us. By following her mentor's advice and trusting in God's guidance, Esther was able to overcome her initial fears and fulfill her purpose. In the same way, we too can find strength and encouragement in the knowledge that God is with us every step of the way.

So, who are we to shy away from the challenge of living with such resolve? Let us be like Esther, willing to surrender our own ambitions and desires in service of a higher purpose. May we seek God's guidance and wisdom at every turn, and trust in His providence to carry us through any trials we may face. Through His grace, we too can be brave and make a lasting impact on the world around us.

Esther's Influence Persists

Remember that one of the two Bible books titled after women is Esther. As aforementioned, she was from a small group that lived in orphanages abroad. She was a regular person whom God transformed into a Persian queen for a reason she could never have anticipated.

Likewise, the same God has plans for your life (Jeremiah 29:11–13) as well.

Esther was able to influence the king and save her people because of her decision to put her faith in God. A Purim feast was held in honor of her courage, and a proclamation was issued, declaring that "these days of Purim should be remembered and honored throughout every generation" from that day forward (Esther 9:28).

Esther's people continue to celebrate Purim today. Her story encourages readers to have faith in God's omnipotence to use anybody who submits to His will and His ways to accomplish His purposes.

Many years ago, when I was a young child sitting around the campfire in the Bahamas, God used Esther's narrative to encourage me to answer the call on my life. Even today, one of my favorite lessons to impart at women's gatherings comes from Esther's life story. I hope God also inspires you. Oh, that every generation of Christians would take a lesson from Esther's determination to live for God's purpose and fortitude and declare, "If I die, I die," but I will serve Christ.

Uncovering Your God-Given Talents

> Every excellent grace and every perfect gift descends from on high, from the Father of lights, with whom there is neither change nor shadow of variation. (James 1:17)

Are you ready to accomplish your mission? Are you ready to enter the destiny that God has traced for you?

These are questions we must ask and answer ourselves because this is the real challenge of our lives: to fulfill our purposes. After being touched by God, after giving Him our hearts, our goal is to do His will and live what He has planned for us.

God has a purpose for you; it is unique and personal to you. My desire as a woman is for you to discover it. As God plans a destiny for your life, He equips you accordingly and gives you everything you need to fulfill it. Stop hesitating and asking yourself questions. You are good at fulfilling your destiny. Your life has a purpose! You are a Christian not only to receive the Word but also to serve God. He doesn't want you to be mere spectators as women. He wants you to be actors!

That's why He gives you talents.

We all have unique gifts, talents, and abilities given to us by our heavenly Father. At birth, we brought these gifts, talents, and abilities with us.

The prophet Moses was a great leader but needed Aaron, his brother, to help him as a spokesman (see Exodus 4:14–16). Some of us are leaders like Moses or good speakers like Aaron. Some of us sing well or play an instrument. Others are good at sports or are gifted with their hands. We may have other talents—for example, understanding others, patience, cheerfulness, or the ability to teach.

We have the responsibility to cultivate the talents we have received. We sometimes think that we don't have many talents or that other people have been given more abilities than us. Sometimes we don't use our talents because we're afraid of failure or criticism. We must not hide our talents. We have to use them. Others can then see our good works and glorify our heavenly Father (see Matthew 5:16).

We must do certain things to cultivate our talents. First, we must discover them. We need to assess ourselves to discover our strengths and abilities. Our families and friends can help us do this. We should also ask our heavenly Father to help us recognize our talents.

Second, we must be willing to invest the time and effort necessary to develop the talent we seek.

Third, we must have faith that our heavenly Father will help us, and we must believe in ourselves.

Fourth, we must acquire the skills necessary to develop our talents. We can do this by taking a class, asking a friend to help us, or reading a book.

Fifth, we must exercise our talents. All talents require effort and work. Mastering a talent is something that has to be earned.

Sixth, we must share our talents with others. When we use our talents, they grow (see Matthew 25:29).

These steps are more accessible if we pray and ask the Lord for help. He wants us to discover our talents and gifts and use them for our purpose in life, as He is always ready to help us.

Talent and Gifts Are Indicators of Life's Purpose

We must know that we all have a purpose to accomplish on this earth. We will accomplish this mission through our areas of competence, which we call gifts and talents.

You cannot claim to be doing a spy mission if you are not a spy first. In the spiritual, it is the same thing. Your talents and gifts are indicators that guide you toward your life purpose. Do you ever feel useless? Unable to accomplish anything? Do you have feelings of boredom that make you feel like you are not passionate about anything? If you recognize yourself in these questions, it means that you have not yet discovered your talents and gifts.

The Holy Spirit gives gifts to each, according to our wills, to build up the church. God gives the gift according to the call we have; that is why we must not envy the gifts of others or see ourselves as superior or inferior. We only flourish if we work in the area of our gifts and talents.

How to Recognize Your Talents as a Woman

Start with the fact that talent is a gift from God. It's a gift that's buried within you and hidden among many other skillful talents. You know how to do several small things simultaneously, especially if you have an advanced education. With all this know-how, you likely no longer know what your true talent is. That's what makes it hard to find.

To recognize our talents, we use the same process as when, for example, we guess which gift a loved one has given us among several other gifts that we have received, when the name of the gift-giver is not written on the gift. When we were children and received presents at Christmas, we had fun guessing which present was from Mom or Dad or the godfather, for example.

Here's what we did: We based our guesses on the tastes,

preferences, and character of the person; sometimes, we even considered the person's profession. For example, my mother-in-law always gave my daughter a spiritual gift, such as a journal or Bible-based books, and my daughter knew immediately that it had come from her. With this process, my daughter almost always managed to guess the giver of her gifts.

We will use the same process to recognize our talents, which are gifts from our Father who is in heaven. The more you come to know the character of God, the easier it will become for you to know with certainty what your talents are. To help you, I will give the criteria to recognize talents, based on some of God's character traits.

Criteria for Recognizing Talents

It's simple.

Divine talent is recognized by three criteria. It is necessary to consider the three criteria together; if one criterion is missing, it's not your talent.

First, you can recognize your talent by your results and success in exercises. For example, if you play football more brilliantly than others, and your results are above average, it means that you have a talent in this area. If you are average in this field, it means that you have little talent in this activity. Here's another example: at school, you performed various activities and were assessed. If you received excellent grades that went beyond mere studying, you were gifted in those subjects. The bottom line is that spectacular results in one area are a sure sign of divine talent because God is perfection. It is one of His characteristics.

The second criterion for recognizing your talent is to list the activities you like to do and that you perform without constraint for unusually long hours. For example, you like to cook; you spend hours cooking without getting tired. When there is a celebration, you volunteer to cook for the guests—without being paid—just because it gives you joy.

The activities that you do out of love and passion are a sign of a talent. Take this second criterion into account to recognize your talent because God is love. In love, there is the principle of the freedom to choose. Free will is a sacrosanct principle with God. God will never give you a talent you don't want to practice. If you don't like what you do as an activity, you have acquired only technical know-how; it is not a divine talent.

The third criterion to consider when recognizing a divine talent is its usefulness for others. God will not give you a talent that does not benefit others. All talents are helpful for other people. If not, it's a hobby and personal entertainment, not a talent.

For example, let's say you like to watch TV or surf Facebook for hours. If this activity fascinates you but brings nothing to others, it is a hobby and not a talent. On the other hand, if you watch TV for hours, and you manage to detect what is wrong with TV programs, and you bring ideas for improvement to the initiators of the TV channel, that is a talent because it helps others.

You may like to make jokes. If it cheers up people and allows them to destress, that is a talent.

God is a gift of self and the provider of all our needs. Because of this characteristic, He fulfills our needs in advance by offering a talent to another who, by exercising it, will fulfill our needs.

Here is how to recognize His talents. Examine yourself, and put all your skills or activities through the lens of the three criteria: (1) excellent results, (2) passion and love for the activity, and (3) useful to others.

Now, I want to give some personal advice. First, talent has to be sought. You must do everything to find it. Behind every talent is a massive influx of success and prosperity, like the biblical characters and the great fortunes of this world. Make the effort to research your talents with perseverance (Matthew 6:32).

Second, if you have several talents, exploit them all. Don't leave even a single talent idle. Imitate King David in the Bible. David had many talents. The Bible said he knew how to play music (the harp), but he also knew how to fight, and he was a leader. David used these talents thoroughly during his life. David composed over one hundred hymns and psalms, which Jews and Christians have continued to use in prayer and song for over two thousand years. He was known not only for his talents as a warrior but also for his talents as a composer and musician. Research and use all your talents.

Third, develop and use your talents. If you don't use them, you will lose them. God Himself will snatch them from you. I refer you to the Parable of the Talents in Matthew 25:14–40.

The fourth and final tip for recognizing your talents is more of a warning: once you have found your talents and put them to use, you undoubtedly will have prosperity but also persecution. Jesus Christ gives us this warning in the following terms:

> Truly I tell you," Jesus replied, "no one who has left home or brothers or sisters or mother or father or children or fields for me and the gospel will fail to receive a hundred times as much in this present age: homes, brothers, sisters, mothers, children and fields—along with persecutions—and in the age to come eternal life. (Mark 10:29-30)

Despite the persecution, you should continue to work on your talents, to improve them, to push them to their maximum, and to polish them as one polishes a precious stone, for the service of God. Your financial resources must be at the service of your talents to make them more efficient. In that way, just like a cut diamond, you will take on more value, and you will become more prosperous.

We have a responsibility to use the talents God has given us. We must not waste them by stifling them or hiding them. We must use them to grow God's kingdom! Otherwise, God will hold us to account, as the master did with his servants.

Now, look at the cross, and ask Jesus the following:

> *Lord, help me to see the gifts and talents that You have put in me and my brothers and sisters. We all have received something from You, and I need not look at my neighbors to compare myself to them because what You have given me is enough to fulfill my destiny.*

CHAPTER 3

EMBRACE YOUR PURPOSE

And we know that all things work together for good
to those who love God, to those who are the called
according to His purpose.

—Romans 8:28

$\mathcal{G}$od put each of us here for a purpose. Serving others is always
a part of what we do. If we serve, we must believe that we are at
the appropriate location and time. In other words, we have to be
conscious of our strategic placement. No matter what situation
we are in right now, we should regard it as an opportunity for
God to reveal His purpose. Here are four strategies to strengthen
your belief in the purpose you were given by God.

1. Consider yourself as well-positioned.

A strategy is a plan or a way to achieve a goal. We have the
privilege of participating in God's strategic plan as believers. The
book of Esther is the ideal example of how one woman's destiny
was incorporated into God's grand plan. Esther was put in a

BRENDA MOUZON, PH.D.

good spot. And when God said, "And who knows but that you have risen to royal position for such a time as this," her cousin Mordecai reminded Esther of this fact. Because of her beauty, others might have assumed she would marry the king. They might have believed that she would become queen due to her cousin's relationship with the king's chamberlain. Esther, however, saw that there was a higher purpose for her life than achieving high status (although she did become queen), enjoying a luxurious lifestyle, and dressing attractively. She knew she was in a unique position to accomplish something that others couldn't.

Are there things you can do for God that others can't because they aren't in your position? When people look at you, they might assume that your education, intelligence, or connections have helped you to get where you are, but our God doesn't operate in that way. Because you are in your position and others are not, you can accomplish things they cannot.

That brings us to our second point—your purpose cannot wait for you to get to your desired destination.

2. Link your purpose to your current situation.

If all you're doing is passing through, you'll never be a person of significance. You are in a unique position to participate in God's plan. Whatever you're doing at the moment is a recipe for success.

The king had not summoned Esther for thirty days at the time of her mission, according to the book of Esther.

Esther held a position in the court, but she did not frequently interact with the king. She did not feel that her position was appropriate. It could have been better if she had spoken to the king more recently. She still held the position of queen, though. Esther didn't attempt to postpone her assignment and wait for a more convenient time. She approached the king at the right

42

moment because she was committed to God's plan to save the Jewish people and was willing to risk her life to do so.

Now let's think about our third point: risk-taking is often necessary for a purpose.

3. Be prepared to take a considerable risk.

Most Christians nowadays don't live in cultures, as Esther did, in which risking their lives is expected of them, but we do have to deal with failure, rejection, and reputational damage. By going to the king without an invitation, Esther risked death. Short of losing her life, she might have been expelled from the king's presence for her wrongdoing in approaching him without invitation. Losing her reputation would have resulted from that.

Although not on the same scale as losing our lives, losing our reputations can be incredibly upsetting when it's unfair and beyond our control. For instance, your friends might not agree with your decision to homeschool your kids, and they no longer respect you. In fact, being rejected by others and losing your reputation frequently go hand in hand.

Esther might have been rejected by the king. The most unsettling of all the risks may be rejection because of our goals. Have you ever been so afraid of being turned down that you talked yourself out of spreading the Gospel, submitting a job application, or taking a course? You even might have felt physically uncomfortable.

To fulfill our goals, we must confront the possibility of rejection. Another risk we must be willing to accept is the impending threat of failure.

Esther's perspective was limited, so failure was a possibility. The king had the option to follow the advice of his counselors and have the Jews executed.

Whether we fail in front of others or not, it is disturbing. Failure may feel like our mission has died if we have been transparent and up front about it. God, however, transcends our shortcomings. His will is centered on our purposes. He makes everything come together for our good. And sometimes, timing is all that's required.

4. Be prepared to wait until the designated hour.

Be mindful that not all of God's purposes are revealed simultaneously. When Esther was supposed to be in the spotlight, she wasn't. She was going about her daily business while secluded with the king's other wives.

Have you ever wondered what God has in store for you while you've wandered through the wilderness of the daily grind? Don't give up or assume you're doing everything incorrectly. Keep your composure, and trust that your mission will become clearer as God's plan takes hold.

The book of Esther is full of mystery, suspense, and romance, but more importantly, it shows what you must do to accept the purpose that God has given you:

- Consider yourself as well-positioned.
- Link your purpose to your present situation.
- Be prepared to take any risk.
- Be prepared to wait until the designated time

Esther saved the nation. What action will you take to live out your purpose today? Encourage yourself to accept your place and function in God's eternal plan.

Deborah: Embracing God's Call

In the days of Shamgar son of Anath, in the days of Jael, the highways were abandoned; travelers took to winding paths. Villagers in Israel would not fight; they held back until I, Deborah, arose, until I arose, a mother in Israel. 'Wake up, wake up, Deborah! Wake up, wake up, break out in song! Arise, Barak! Take captive your captives, son of Abinoam.' (Judges 5:6–7, 12)

The Bible tells the story of Deborah and demonstrates how the Lord sometimes calls ordinary people to do extraordinary things that are only possible when the Spirit is present. This Bible study of Judges 4–5 examines the lessons that Deborah can teach us about our calling and the influence of the Holy Spirit. First, let's pray the following prayer:

I give thanks to the Lord that He enjoys working mighty deeds through ordinary people like me. Release me, Lord, from any obstacles that I, others, or the enemy has placed on my life that have prevented me from achieving the wonderful goals You have for me so that I might arise and shine for Your glory. In Jesus's name, Amen.

The beginning of Deborah's story in Judges 4–5 is similar to many other stories in the book of Judges: after the Israelites disobeyed the Lord, the Israelite leader sold them to King Jabin of Canaan. The Israelites called out to the Lord for assistance after this continued for twenty years. Deborah was serving as the nation's judge at the time. She sent for Israel's army commander Barak and ordered him to engage Sisera's army, which was led by Jabin. Barak stated that he would only travel if Deborah accompanied him. Deborah concurred but informed Barak that a woman would be given control of Sisera by the Lord, so he would not receive the distinction.

The Lord decimated Sisera's army as Barak's army advanced, and Sisera fled on foot. Due to a partnership between King Jabin and Heber's family, Sisera visited Jael, Heber's wife, in her tent. Jael welcomed Sisera inside and gave him drinks. Sisera passed out from exhaustion. Jael killed Sisera by driving a tent peg into his skull. King Jabin was defeated after a long battle by the

Israelites. Israel enjoyed peace for forty years after Deborah and Barak performed a hymn of gratitude.

Greater Depth

Deborah was a busy woman. She held court under the Palm of Deborah between Ramah and Bethel in the hills of Ephraim, according to Judges 4:5, and the Israelites went up to her to settle their issues. Deborah possessed a tremendous amount of discernment, wisdom, and revelation. She also possessed a prophetic gift, which included knowing the Lord's appointed times and seasons. She was able to plainly hear the Lord's voice.

Judges 5:12, however, commands Deborah to "wake up, wake up! Wake up, awaken, and start singing! Barak, get up! Son of Abinoam, take your prisoners into captivity." To recognize a fresh revelation and dimension of their callings, Deborah and Barak needed to "wake up and arise." The Lord warned them to be on guard and to pay attention because He was going to act in a remarkable fashion.

> Villagers in Israel would not fight; they withheld themselves until I, Deborah, a mother in Israel, rose. (Judges 5:7)

Deborah might have legally referred to herself as a judge, prophetess, deliverer, intercessor, or worshipper, but she decided to call herself a mother instead. She was a mother first and foremost. That much is obvious. She was a mother "in Israel," but she was also a mother "over Israel," so it's unclear who her children were (it can be translated both ways). She viewed all of Israel as her children and desired both her actual and figurative children to live in peace and safety.

The verse states that until Deborah "arose," no one in Israel would battle. Twenty years of enslavement had worn down the Israelites. They were too worn out and defeated to engage in combat. The Lord selected Deborah to serve as their source of motivation. Nothing would have changed if she hadn't followed the Lord's instructions and done as He commanded. She encouraged Barak to recruit an army by using the position of trust and power she had been granted as a judge.

Deborah was a warrior who worshipped. She could be obedient to whatever the Lord asked her to do because of the inspiration and power she found in worship. Deborah would not have gone through all the experiences that led to the Lord using her to free Israel from slavery if she had taken a back seat in her life. She wouldn't have had the knowledge and insight to decide conflicts. As an intercessor, she would not have been aware of the Lord's tactical combat plans. She would not have extended the loving heart of her maternal grandmother to include all of Israel. She wouldn't have empowered and healed an entire nation.

The order given to Barak was, "Arise and take captive your captives" (Judges 5:12). Barak was hesitant to go into combat without Deborah, but in the end, he was willing to muster an army and follow Deborah's instructions. This obedience also was required to carry out the Lord's plans.

Without mentioning Jael, another woman who stepped up to physically stake her place in history, Deborah's story would fall short. Jael took the necessary action because she was in the right place at the right time. Deborah described Jael as "most blessed of tent-dwelling women" (Judges 5:24). Jael, a housewife, was crucial to winning the war.

Both She and I Receive Calls

I would like to encourage you. We frequently are reluctant to leave our comfort zones and fulfill the Lord's calling. Most of us would say a firm no if the Lord revealed His complete plan for our lives in advance—it's a blessing that He doesn't.

Don't believe the lie that the devil tells you—that God will never use you to do great things. Don't let your concern for what people might think prevent you from following God or from being used to do incredible things. The Lord prepared Deborah in her place of worship in secret, which increased her trust in her ability to discern God's voice. As she determined when it was appropriate to go to war, her intentional relationship with God through worship provided her courage.

The Lord will treat us in the same way. God will lead us to clarity on our call as we grow closer to Him. God repeatedly reaffirms us in a variety of ways. We are starting on an amazing path of serving the Lord here on earth as followers of Christ.

It's time for you, woman of God, to step forth in courage and perform the extraordinary purpose to which you have been called. Will you embrace the challenge to be a light in the darkness for the kingdom of God, wherever the Lord has placed you? Will you persuade others to follow that example? Get up and reflect the light of God wherever you go! It's time to quit hiding and acting timidly because you represent the hope that this world desperately needs—the hope of Jesus Christ. Waiting for you to obey is a dying, forlorn world. Trust that God has the best plan for you, and follow Him to the place where He is at work.

CHAPTER 4

THE PASSION PRINCIPLE

And whatever you do, do it heartily, as to the Lord
and not to men, knowing that from the Lord you will
receive the reward of the inheritance; for you serve the
Lord Christ.

—Colossians 3:23–24

*T*he passion principle is the "whatsoever principle." Paul declared
to the Colossians, "Whatever you do, do it heartily as to the Lord
and not to men" (Colossians 3:23). This principle includes all our
lives. We're to do everything wholeheartedly—full of joy, full of
passion!

Passion gives the drive. Passion sets the speed. The more
passionate you are, the more fervent you are. Your passions
are those things you appreciate and love to do—activities that
easily interest you and provide delight to your day. Therefore,
understanding your passions is extremely important and worth
your effort.

One approach for uncovering your passion is to write a list
of the activities you love to do. Here are three ways you may
construct that list and get on with finding that passion:

1. Make a list of the everyday activities you require to feel pleased. This is crucial, as you'll then be aware of what you intentionally want to achieve every day. The activities you enjoy help you to clearly realize who you are.
2. List the daily activities you want to engage in that are neither necessary nor significant. This provides an opportunity to distinguish essential from unimportant information. This could make a significant difference in how straightforward and uncluttered your life is.
3. Make a list of the things you would or shouldn't do if you wanted to continue being amazing and passionate about your work or career. Just let them go. When you establish clear boundaries in your life, you can better identify and quickly remedy any errors you may make.

Another method to get things going is to take a quick trip down memory lane. Consider the various roles you have held or performed throughout your life. What was successful and for whom? Which caught your attention more? What could you have lacked at this time?

Fundamental Idea of Having Passion for Your Vision

- Without passion, success is impossible.
- Those who are passionate about something have found something greater than life itself.
- Passion is a prerequisite for vision.
- Trials will always put a vision to the test.
- One sign of the passion's legitimacy is its adherence to the vision.
- Passion indicates that, despite difficulties, what you believe is more important than what you see.
- Someone with passion is constantly ready to realize his or her vision.

Your passion helps you to remain focused on your goal.

There will be opposition as you carry out your vision, so please be aware. Only by being passionate about your vision can you overcome such opposition. When your desire is important to you, you will be able to face challenges head-on. Remember that perseverance will keep you moving forward, but perseverance needs passion to thrive.

A passionate woman always wants to realize her dreams. You will be rewarded if you maintain your vision. As you work toward realizing your vision and ambition, you will face challenges and tests.

Please remember that passion helps you stay focused. Fighting, arguing, squabbling, whispering, backbiting, and complaining frequently occur when there is no vision. When churches are overflowing with complaints, that is a sign that the vision has faded. When people are preoccupied with the vision, however, they have no time for idle chatter, hostility toward the pastor, or criticism of the sermon.

Marriages can exhibit the same problem. I have observed this in my previous relationships. Couples lose their shared vision, which is why marriages have many issues. It will take time to rekindle our passion for cooperating toward a common goal and vision. If you have discovered your passion, stay by it, and learn to focus and develop it daily. You will be rewarded if you maintain your vision.

The Five Principles of Success

If you allow it, the art of success is fundamentally simple. Far too frequently, some people complicate what success is and how it might be attained. Success is not difficult to accomplish; you just need to put in time and effort over an extended period.

There are fundamental ideas that you should apply to your

life, whether you're an entrepreneur or just trying to succeed in life. Put the following success principles into practice—that's all you ever need to do.

1. Your suffering leads to your prosperity.

Although it doesn't seem like the first principle will help you succeed, it is the most crucial of all. Regardless of where you look, any fantastic story, inspirational figure, or person who has accomplished the impossible has had to overcome some kind of adversity or pain. Your success may be fueled by a start-up, family dissolution, unsuccessful marriage, connection, or even a disaster. Even though it may feel like nothing is working out for you right now, the pain will ultimately lead to your achievement. Your prospects of success are limited if you never go through hardship or a serious battle.

The suffering will cause you to reconsider all you have done thus far and break your routine. You may lack the motivation and ambition to succeed. As long as you understand the situation's message, success is around the corner when you see the pain coming.

2. All that matters is having a passion for life.

You may get the impression that someone is lifeless when she lacks passion. Once you get to know someone who lives life to the fullest, you'll realize that passion is what gives her life. When the passion is gone, she loses life and returns to being ordinary. We often discuss passion, but we never find it. If there is one thing that we are destined to find in life, it would be our passion. We wake up early in the morning and stay up late at night because of it. We continually take notes on our smartphones about it and discuss it the most. Do you know that one thing that sends shivers down your spine? You will succeed if you can discover what that passion is for you. All that's left to do is use it and make it your obsession, once it's been unlocked.

In looking back on my life, I have learned that I frequently gave up on my passion just when I was about to achieve something remarkable. Not this time, though. I am living with my passion as if it's my final chance at doing it.

Make finding your purpose your top priority. Even if it takes some time, the success principle is where all other ideas originate.

3. Be thankful.

We can all choose what to do when we wake up. Being thankful for what you have right now is the one decision you should make daily. Be thankful that if you are struggling to find success, you can just switch on a movie to see others pursuing their dreams and succeeding; you can then apply the techniques from the movie to your situation.

Be thankful that you have the freedom to begin anything new whenever you like. With your dream and what you are good at, you have the chance to motivate others. Just a smile or the smallest action can radically alter how someone is feeling. All of the individuals you respect express gratitude, so you should do the same. Don't be frightened to simply be content with your current situation. Keep doing what you're doing, be persistent, and don't give up.

4. Believe in yourself—you have amazing things in you.

We are all meant for greatness, but you must first believe this statement to fully utilize the power of this success principle. Once you believe you can succeed, all it takes is determination. If you believe you will be average, you will be, but if you feel you will be excellent at something, you will eventually become so.

Although we all need to get moving right now, none of us has to stay ordinary. To achieve an objective, we must act.

In my own life, I firmly believe that I can encourage others through my work, and this confidence will never waver. No matter how stupid or uninspiring others may think I am, I know that my thoughts will determine how my future turns out. Even at my lowest, when I believe nobody is listening, when they don't acknowledge me, or when they don't like my Facebook posts, people are still observing me at my finest.

5. Fire up.

Fire up is the simplest of the success principles. This may seem like a meaningless phrase, but it packs a significant punch. *Fire up* is a metaphor for living life to its fullest potential. Change your posture, speech pattern, attire, and method of standing, as well as your body language. Act as if a football coach is yelling in your ear to try harder and be more passionate in all that you do.

My friend from high school, who everyone liked because he always was fun to be around, coined the simple expression "fire up." He would scream at people in a positive way and let everyone see how happy he was, which made everyone else feel good.

You must be passionate and vulnerable to lead others and have them follow your example. Show people all parts of you, not just the flawless facets that many individuals use to represent who they are on social media.

Your circumstances will change when you truly begin to live at your peak, and people will be drawn to you. During a sales pitch, you will be more convincing and secure than ever. If you continue down this route, you might even become a world leader, and you will influence one.

CHAPTER 5

ROADBLOCKS ON THE
ROAD TO PURPOSE

$\mathcal{F}$inding your purpose is not always easy—finding my own purpose came out of a painful business failure. In fact, the process can be so tricky that many don't even bother to search for it. Others don't want to be responsible for what they find. Still others don't want to be restricted because they enjoy freelancing, doing a little of this and a little of that. Let's look at some of the roadblocks you may encounter as you seek to find and clarify your purpose.

Don't confuse "tent-making" with your purpose. I asked a young lady one time what her purpose was, and she responded without thought, "I'm a secretary." Don't assume that your job is your purpose. You're undoubtedly performing a job that pays your bills, but that doesn't mean you should take your identity from it.

William Carey, the great missionary pioneer, once said, "My business is to witness for Christ. I make shoes to pay my expenses. If people had asked Paul what his purpose was, I doubt that he would have responded, 'I'm a tentmaker.'" He did make tents, but his purpose was to preach to the Gentiles. He used tent-making to accomplish his purpose.

Nehemiah wasn't a butler; he was the rebuilder of Jerusalem. Once you see your purpose, it will help you endure a job that may be a source of frustration for you. Having a proper understanding of your purpose will keep you from feeling as if you're not serving the Lord just because you're employed in a secular position.

A woman writer worked for a Christian magazine years ago, and she took a standardized spiritual-gifts test because she was trying to clarify her purpose. Her test results showed that she was firm in missions and hospitality (which confirmed what she always enjoyed doing), which stimulated her thinking. She asked herself how she could fulfill her purpose as a missionary while employed in Mobile. The Lord soon showed her how to serve college students from foreign countries, and she began to specifically target students from Mainland China.

Today, she continues to fulfill her purpose to the Chinese in Florida, where she is a freelance writer. She has edited a newspaper directed at Chinese students and also writes articles and books that serve to heighten people's awareness of the needs and opportunities of Chinese missions. She doesn't see herself primarily as a writer, although that's how she makes her living. She's a missionary and has found creative, Spirit-led ways to do what she was born to do.

Married women are particularly vulnerable to this identity crisis because they tend to draw their purpose from their day-to-day activities and routine. Housekeeping and raising children can fall under the category of "tent-making." That's what consumes most of a homemaker's time, but are those activities her divine purpose?

Anna found herself in this situation in Luke 2:36–38. She was married for seven years when her husband died, but her purpose didn't die with him. Instead, she served in the temple and "worshiped night and day, fasting and praying." Anna was eighty-four years old when Mary and Joseph came to the temple.

She ministered effectively and waited to see the hope of Israel. Women have purpose before they meet their spouses and after they have children.

Don't underestimate your ability to work. The forty-hour workweek is a modern phenomenon, a product of technology and union negotiations. If you work in the energy and power of God, you can do more than you ever thought possible! You can work sixteen-hour days and still be effective.

Paul preached all night on at least one occasion because his purpose compelled him to move on the next day. During that sermon, a young man sank into a deep sleep and fell to the ground from the third story because of preaching so long (see Acts 20). But Paul raised him and kept functioning in his purpose of preaching to the Gentiles. Paul wrote that he endured "in hard work, sleepless nights and hunger" (2 Corinthians 6:5).

Years ago, a man was pastoring a church of fifty people. That kept him busy, but he also served as a church administrator. In addition, he had family responsibilities and was involved in several community service projects. Despite of all that, he was asked to consider being the administrator for another ministry without relinquishing any of the responsibilities he already had. There was no way he could do it all—or so he thought.

He sought the Lord about his duties and what he should eliminate. One morning, he awoke with "1 Corinthians 15:10" on his mind. He didn't know what the verse said, and he hadn't been reading Corinthians lately. He went right to the Bible and found the answer to the question he had been asking God:

> But by the grace of God I am what I am, and His grace which was bestowed upon me was not in vain; but I labored more abundantly than they all yet not I, but the grace of God which was with me. (1 Corinthians 15:10)

The Lord clearly was telling him that there wasn't going to

be any less to do. In fact, He increased the man's duties without taking any away. He wanted to teach him how to handle an enlarged sphere!

If God wants you to go back to school, for instance, don't say, "I can't because classes are at night, and I will be away from my family. It will cut into this or that." Go to school. You may be concerned that you won't have time to study, but you won't know that for sure until you get into it.

It's hard, but it can be done. If I did it, so can you because the same grace is available to you. Take a look at 1 Corinthians 3:13—"His work will be shown for what it is." The word *work* is the Greek word *kopos*. It literally means "a beating of breast with grief." It also translates as "intense labor united with toil and trouble." That is what comes with purpose and hard work with some measure of trouble.

A few years ago, an issue of *Christian History* magazine was devoted to "The Golden Age of Hymns" and featured articles about the great hymn writers of the past. One paragraph that captured my attention told of William Cowper, who composed sixty-eight hymns in his lifetime; John Newton, who wrote 280; Philip Doddridge, who produced almost 400; and Isaac Watts, who wrote 697 hymns. Charles Wesley, however, wrote 898 hymns! Wesley didn't have a computer, FAX machine, or telephone. He wrote some hymns while on horseback, going from one revival meeting to the next. Charles Wesley was a man who knew his purpose. He was effective and worked long and hard, and he has impacted many people for over two hundred years!

Don't pursue or pay for the purpose that you want to have. That is a serious hindrance to finding your true purpose. Churches sometimes get torn apart because the associate pastor wants to be the pastor, or the youth director wants more responsibility. I've seen men and women quit their jobs because they felt those jobs weren't spiritual enough.

You sincerely can be wrong. Sincerity is not the judge of accuracy. This happened to the apostle Paul.

> A man named Ananias came to see me. He was a devout observer of the law and highly respected by all the Jews living there. He stood beside me and said, "Brother Saul, receive your sight!" And at that very moment I was able to see him. Then he said, "The God of our fathers has chosen you to know his will and to see the Righteous One and to hear words from his mouth. You will be his witness to all men of what you have seen and heard. And now what are you waiting for? Get up, be baptized and wash your Sins away, calling on his name." When I returned to Jerusalem and was praying at the temple, I fell into a trance and saw the Lord speaking'. "Quick.' he said to me. "Leave Jerusalem immediately, because they will not accept your testimony about me." "Lord," I replied, "these men know that I went from one synagogue to another to imprison and beat those who believe in you. And when the blood of your martyr Stephen was shed, I stood there giving my approval and guarding the clothes of those 'who were killing him." Then the Lord said to me, "Go; I will send you far away to the Gentiles." (Acts 33:12–21)

What was Paul doing in Jerusalem? I believe he was pursuing the purpose he wanted to have. To paraphrase Paul, he said, "God's going to send me to my people, the Jews. I am a Jew. I'm already here in the temple. They all know I persecuted the disciples. They will know something happened on the road. You see, Lord, this is what I want to do for You. This is where You can best use me, and it makes the most sense to me. And by the way, this is also where I feel most comfortable."

God responded to Paul by ordering him to leave Jerusalem. It would have cost Paul his life to stay there, and it would cost him something to be involved in a purpose or pursuit not ordained by God—he would be busy but not effective.

> He who works his land will have abundant food, but the
> one who chases fantasies will have his fill of poverty.
> (Proverbs 28:19)

You have a plot of land to work. It belongs to you and you alone. If you work it, God will give you all that you need to get the job done. Any other field is a fantasy for you and will trap you in unfruitful busyness.

Wrong Attitudes

It's so easy to get distracted in today's world. The lure of money, success, and materialism can keep you from devoting yourself to your purpose. As mentioned, you're a hireling if you work for money, no matter what your job. You should work to help establish and strengthen God's kingdom wherever He sends you. Your provision is His responsibility. He is committed to providing for you in any and every situation. Don't let money, pride, success, fear, the acclaim of others, or ministry success keep you from fulfilling your purpose. A correct attitude is essential if you are to find your mission. When you find it, take whatever steps are necessary to carry it out.

Don't focus on your purpose at the expense of your relationship with the Lord. In Acts 13, Saul was finally released to the Gentiles. Acts 13:2 says, "The Holy Spirit said, 'Set apart for me Barnabas and Saul.'" The Greek phrase *set apart for me* is in the middle voice, which can denote someone doing something to oneself. The middle voice in this verse denotes that the Holy Spirit was calling them to their purpose by calling them to Himself. Your revealed purpose should never take on greater importance than your relationship with the Lord. If it fits, God will resist you until your priorities are correct.

Paul understood this and wrote about it to the Philippian church.

> For me, to live is Christ and to die is gain. If I am to go on living in the body, this will mean fruitful (effective) labor for me. Yet what shall I choose? I do not know! I am torn between the two: I desire to depart and be with Christ, Christ, which is better by far; but it is more necessary for you that I remain in the body. (Philippians 1:21–24)

As important as Paul's mission was, he was ready to leave it to be with the Lord, for that was "better." He was content to stay on because it was useful to many, but he was ready to leave it at any time. That attitude enabled Paul to be even more effective, since his focus was on the Lord and not on ministry or the people.

God doesn't need you. He does, however, choose to use you. Don't take yourself too seriously! After all, God spoke to Balaam through a donkey, and He can get praise from rocks if He so desires. Take God seriously, and you will develop an effective lifestyle. Take yourself too seriously, and you will become busy but not effective.

If you keep an eye out for these roadblocks, your journey on the road to clearly defining your purpose will be a smooth one.

CHAPTER 6

A WOMAN OF FAITH AND PRAYER

$\mathcal{M}$any women of faith in the Bible led lives of prayer. In the following, we want to look at Hannah, the mother of Samuel. In the first book of Samuel, we are told two of her prayers. In one case, we can speak of prayer; in the other case, of praise.

Hannah's Prayer in 1 Samuel 1

Hannah's situation is well known to most of us. She suffered from her childlessness and the contempt and ridicule of Peninnah, her husband, Elkanah's, second wife. Where should she turn with all her troubles? Sure, her husband, Elkanah, loved her and tried to comfort her as best he could. But only one could really understand the deepest need of her injured and wounded soul—Jehovah, the God of Israel. We see her as a woman "bitter in spirit, and she entreated Jehovah and wept greatly" (1 Samuel 1:10).

She expressed what she did with the following words in this prayer and supplication: "I poured out my soul before God" (1 Samuel 1:15). All believers today have the privilege of pouring out their souls before God. How could it be otherwise, as we know our God in a much deeper, more intimate way—as God and Father of our Lord Jesus Christ? Our Lord Himself made His own say, "My Father; your Father." The apostle Paul urged believers to make their requests in everything known to God through prayer and supplication with thanksgiving, like Hannah (Philippians 4:6).

What would be the result of such fervent prayer? The immediate hearing of and change in our situations? Scripture gives us a different answer:

> The peace of God, which surpasses all understanding,
> will guard your hearts and your minds in Christ Jesus.
> (Philippians 4:7)

Isn't that precisely what we find in Hannah, too?

> And the woman went her way and ate, and her face was
> no longer the same. (1 Samuel 1:18)

Her external circumstances were still the same at that point, but the inner peace of God had moved into her soul, which was also visible in her changed appearance. Her "bitter disposition" had been visible to everyone until then, but the peace of God that filled her was also felt by others.

If we look at Hannah's first prayer, we find something that continues in her second prayer. She was familiar with the Word of God—as far as it was known in her day—and the Word of God influenced and shaped her prayer life. Here, too, Hannah can be a role model for us. In this context, consider only the following three points:

1. When she sought the face of her God as a childless woman, she knew that Sarah, Rebekah, and Rachel had been in the same situation before her and that their help had come from the God of Abraham, Isaac, and Jacob, who was also their God.

2. Certainly, Hannah—that faithful, godly woman—also felt the need of a deliverer for the people of Israel in Eli's day. In the history of God's people, hadn't there already been a childless woman who, as a special grace of God, was allowed to give birth to a Samson, the deliverer from the Philistines? Couldn't she trust that her unchanging God could do the same now?

3. Hannah made a vow to give back her son, whom God would give her, to serve God. She wanted to offer what she had asked of God as a sacrifice. Was she thinking of the progenitor of her people, Abraham, who also sacrificed his long-awaited son to God?

In all, we see that Hannah was a woman of faith and prayer who did not see herself as the center of her prayers. Ultimately, the glorification and glory of God was always before her eyes. Granting her request for a son should not be primarily for her pleasure or to end her hurt. No, this son was to serve God and to be a Nazarite of God in the midst of utter corruption (cf. 1 Samuel 1:11).

Hannah's Praise in 1 Samuel 2

Hannah prays again, but now it is not a matter of requests; her prayer is in praise of the person and action of God.

We can divide this praise into three sections:

1. She extols the nature of God (1 Samuel 2:1–3).
2. She describes God's actions (verses 4–8).
3. She finally casts a prophetic glimpse of the future, culminating in the exaltation of His anointed (verses 9–10).

Hannah describes six qualities of God's characteristics.

1. **He is the Savior.** "For I rejoice in your salvation." She had experienced this herself when God delivered her from her position of shame and contempt. We don't read anything about "bitter spirit" or "spilling out the soul." On the contrary, their hearts rejoiced, their mouths were opened wide, and joy filled their hearts.

2. **God is holy.** "There is none holy like Jehovah." In saying this, Hannah also makes it clear that the decay, decline, and evil associated with the tabernacle and priesthood of her day are inconsistent with this characteristic of God.

3. **God is the only true God.** "For there is none but you." In view of the increasing idolatry among her people, Hannah makes a clear confession to the one God of Israel.

4. **God is trustworthy.** "And no rock is like our God." This "rock of eternity" has always been the unshakable foundation of trust in faith.

5. **God is omniscient.** "For Jehovah is a God of knowledge." Nothing that happened in Israel at that time, whether open or hidden, was hidden from the eyes of the "perfect in knowledge" (Job 37:16).

6. **God is the judge of all.** "By him are actions weighed." God has knowledge of all things and judges all things according to His divine, perfect, and just judgment.

The characteristics of God never change. What we find in the Old Testament is the same in the New Testament. One scripture should suffice for each. The interested Bible reader will easily find more.

> God, who raises the dead, who saved us from so great death and is saving us, in whom we have put our hope, that He will also continue to deliver us. (2 Corinthians 1:9–10)

As he who called you is Holy, so are you also Holy in all your ways. (1 Peter 1:15)

In the beginning was the Word, and the Word was with God, and the Word was God. (John 1:1)

That we might not trust in ourselves, but in God. (2 Corinthians 1:9)

And no creature is invisible before him, but everything is plain and revealed in the sight of him with whom we are dealing. (Hebrews 4:13)

From now on the crown of righteousness is ready for me, which the Lord, the Just Judge, will give me as a reward in that day. (2 Timothy 4:8)

In this prayer, too, Hannah was able to draw on examples from the history of God with His people and in His Word. God is a savior and liberator, which became clear in the liberation of Israel from Egypt. Leviticus contains clear teachings that God is holy. It is repeatedly pointed out in both Exodus and Deuteronomy that God is one. Moses had already spoken of God as a rock (Deuteronomy 32:4–15).

The omniscience of God, even of hidden things, was evident at least since the days of Achan (Joshua 7). What is probably the oldest book in the Bible also speaks of God's judging scale (Job 31:6).

From the prayer life of this faithful Israelite, which God has recorded for us for our instruction, we may draw two lessons for our own benefit:

We can come to God in prayer with all our needs and sorrows, whether it is in our personal lives, in family life, or in the common life of God's people. He hears us; He hears us in His time and in His perfect way. But most importantly, when we bring our concerns to Him, the peace of God will come upon us and guard our hearts and minds in Christ Jesus.

We, however, do not want to invoke God only when we have a personal concern. Instead, like Hannah, we may fellowship with Him in prayer and express adoration before Him; the beauties, glories, and characteristics of His person have become precious to us.

The Importance of a Woman's Prayer

1. She has the ability to make bad situations better. A praying woman resembles the biblical prophetesses Deborah and Queen Esther. They were prayer tigers who controlled the culture during their reigns. Imagine a lady who stood out in the land when all politeness ended, as Deborah did among a million men.

   Until she got up, nothing was happening in her time.

   > Israeli villagers refrained from fighting until I, Deborah, a mother in Israel, rose to my feet. (Judges 5:7)

   A woman of prayer transformed her family's situation for the better. She was a fighter and a chain-breaker.

2. A woman who prays carries the Holy Ghost's stamp and the mark of possession (Galatians 6:17). How does this mark function? The symbol resembles an insignia. It serves as an ownership mark similar to a trademark. This mark was on the apostle Paul. When his assailants grew numerous, he sternly warned them,

   > From now on, let no one worry you; for I carry on my body the markings of Jesus. (Galatians 6:17)

Her offspring have the seal and code of the Holy Spirit, making her like a seal to her family.

Using a student's confession as an example. I've heard demon-possessed children confess that they didn't hurt other kids because their parents were prayerful people or because their mothers were praying tigers.

These are not jokes. The women passed on this fire and these laws to their offspring, making them impervious to the agents of the kingdom of darkness.

3. A woman who prays is like a lion. She is as brave as the biblical Esther. Through prayer, she rouses God's lion nature. Her offspring consist of lions and lionesses. Her family can withstand anything.

4. The realm of evil cannot reach her. She doesn't lose anything. A woman who is pleading has the ministry of Jesus. She fervently protects all that is hers. We observed the situation with the missionary's numerous children and the wicked rich man who attempted to use them in ritualistic money-making.

5. A praying woman in Israel is a mother, according to Judges 5:1–7 and Esther 4:15–17; 6:1. The world around her is constantly in motion. She is a problem-solver.

CHAPTER 7

WHAT ARE YOU TOLERATING THAT IS HINDERING YOUR FLOW?

> Now I urge you, brethren, note those who cause divisions and offenses, contrary to the doctrine which you learned, and avoid them.
>
> —Romans 16:17

*W*omen, especially Christian women, should be happy! Why? God has shown them a tremendous amount of glory. They were chosen by the Triune God from all time and all people, not because of anything special about them but because of His tremendous love. He has given them great honor by appointing them as queens and mothers. In other words, they are a royal priesthood.

According to the apostle Peter,

> You also, as living stones, are being built up a spiritual house, a holy priesthood, to offer up spiritual sacrifices acceptable to God through Jesus Christ. ... But you are a chosen generation, a royal priesthood, a holy nation, His own special people, that you may proclaim the

praises of Him who called you out of darkness into His
marvelous light. (1 Peter 2:5, 9)

You are being built into a spiritual home to be a holy
priesthood, giving spiritual sacrifices acceptable to God through
Jesus Christ. And since followers of Jesus Christ are promoted to
the status of honor, they no longer require human priests to serve
as their intermediaries with God.

No, we have open access to God's holiness. Even if we
Christians were nothing before, we are now somebody, and we
may celebrate this honor that God has given to everyone who has
accepted the gospel and placed their faith in Jesus Christ.

No matter our situations in life or exterior characteristics,
like color, gender, or race, every believer woman is a queen and
a mother.

There is neither Jew nor Greek, there is neither slave
nor free, there is neither male nor female; for you are
all one in Christ Jesus. (Galatians 3:28)

By divine decree, we are all mothers of the house of God. God
expects you to live a fulfilling life, be successful in every aspect of
your journey, be successful in your business, and to accomplish
your life's purpose, as stated in this scripture. Peter the apostle
stated, "If indeed you have tasted that the Lord is gracious"
(1 Peter 2:3). You have experienced the saving grace of God,
and you have turned from the evil of the past to Jesus, who has
forgiven your sins, written your name in the book of life, changed
your life, and made you a new creation by grace, to advance you
both in the world and in the kingdom of God.

Occasionally, these promises fail to materialize in our lives
due to negative attitudes or actions. If we want to develop as
spiritual or business persons; if we want to succeed in our careers,
studies, society, and marriages; or if we want to lead, we must set
aside some things.

> Therefore we also, since we are surrounded by so great
> a cloud of witnesses, let us lay aside every weight, and
> the sin which so easily ensnares us, and let us run with
> endurance the race that is set before us. (Hebrews
> 12:1)

God is telling you through His Word to lay away anything that will prevent you from growing. Consider all the biblical heroes of faith, but there are some people you won't find in the Hall of Fame because they weren't willing to set some things aside. Esau and Balaam lacked endurance. Saul and Absalom lacked patience. Lot's wife loved worldly attachment.

There are some things we should set aside if we want to reach the chapter of life and spend all eternity with the Lord in heaven. Judas Iscariot did not put an end to his covetousness. Demas (in the book of Philemon) received much of the Word of God from the apostle Paul as his companion, but he did not put an end to his love for the world. King Ahab did not put an end to his renowned lifestyle, nor did his wife, Jezebel, put an end to her iniquity. Lay down anything today that hinders your progress, shortens your blessings, prevents you from fulfilling your life's purpose, diverts your focus from the Lord, and restricts your concentration.

The apostle Paul states,

> Examine yourselves as to whether you are in the faith.
> Test yourselves. Do you not know yourselves, that Jesus
> Christ is in you?—unless indeed you are disqualified.
> (2 Corinthians 13:5)

Paul is saying that every man and woman should examine himself or herself for the things that cause this limitation. What are these things that cause us not to reach our purpose in life? What are these things that cause setbacks in business and are unfruitful in marriage? What are these things that limit our growth and success in life? No matter what kind of success we desire, we should never put up with certain things, as they will limit our growth, confidence, commitment, and productivity. Everybody has shortcomings, but we may not know how simple it is to fix them. Here are some things we need to stop tolerating if we want to perform better and be more successful.

Lack of a Life Purpose and Plan

A life plan requires time, energy, and labor to create. Making a life plan would be another task on our long list of things to do if we didn't comprehend the advantages or reasons behind it. God is able to take us by the hand and guide us because He appreciates our ability to see to the future, plan with Him, and carry things out. Trauma and loss have a way of keeping us imprisoned. Personally, I endured because of my life purpose.

Each person has a plan for you. Your cable TV provider has a plan for you because you may boost their revenue this year. Your internet provider has a plan for you because they are aware that you cannot survive without their service. Your landlord has a plan for you. Your butcher has a plan for you. Your manager has a plan for you. You are part of Mark Zuckerberg's plan because he knows you will use Facebook and contribute to the growth of his business.

But do you have a plan for yourself?

You must have a plan for yourself if you want to succeed. You naturally plan to fail if you don't have a plan for success. You must understand your particular purpose for getting up every day. You must have a goal and a plan for your life. People who are successful plan their lives, stick to a budget, and have goals and dreams.

You need to have a solid plan and a sense of direction in order to achieve in life. Any road will do if we don't know where we're going. It is challenging to achieve meaningful and rewarding success until we have established what success looks like for us.

A basic necessity for consistent, long-term success is having a life plan.

Toxic Relationships.

Toxic simply implies "poisonous." Toxic relationships damage our ability to enjoy another person and keep our peace. A poisonous relationship will leave you feeling worn out, irritated, and occasionally depressed. Business alliances, sports teams, and families, of course, can all be negatively impacted by toxic relationships.

A certain amount of discord in a relationship is acceptable, yet some people poison every relationship, preventing healthy give-and-take. The relationship is entirely skewed to the toxic person's advantage. People who are toxic are extremely egocentric and only consider what they want right now.

Philippians 2:3–4 states, "Do nothing out of selfish ambition or vain conceit." Instead, you are called to practice humility and place the needs of others above your own. Focus on each other's interests rather than your own. Although toxic people may give the impression that they are helping others, they always have another goal in mind that will be to their advantage.

Stop interacting with the incorrect people. Life is too short to waste time with toxic people. The people in your life should encourage, assist, and support you. If not, they're probably making you feel uneasy, which is something you shouldn't have to put up with. You need relationships that will make you feel good about yourself, if you want to succeed.

Lack of Mentors or Role Models from Whom to Learn

A *mentor* is described as "a knowledgeable and dependable counselor or teacher." Despite the absence of the word *mentoring* in the Bible, it does include several examples of mentoring. Moses received guidance from his father-in-law, Jethro (Exodus 18). Eli and Samuel had a mentorship relationship that helped Samuel get ready for the duties and responsibilities that would fall to him once Eli passed away (1 Samuel 1–4). Jesus mentored His disciples (Luke 9), and Barnabas and Paul were also excellent mentors (Acts 9–15). Jesus was very explicit about His mentoring approach. He led so that we could follow.

> If someone wants to follow me, he or she should deny themselves, take up their cross, and do so. (Matthew 16:24)

The apostle Paul described mentoring as his style of leadership in very simple terms:

> Follow my example as I follow Christ's example. (1 Corinthians 11:1)

> Put into effect all you've learned, heard, or seen about me or in me. (Philippians 4:9a)

Basically, he is saying, "Let me be your mentor. Let me be an example for you." He exhorts the Thessalonian new Christians to "follow our example" (2 Thessalonians 3:7).

Believing that we are capable of doing everything on our own is arrogant. The fact is that whatever we are trying to accomplish, someone has already done it, or there are individuals who can help us. Success and growth fundamentally depend on our willingness to always be a learner or student.

Procrastination

> Give no sleep to your eyes, Nor slumber to your eyelids. (Proverbs 6:4)

It is never a good idea to be a procrastinating person, especially if it develops into a habit. Procrastination begins with one item and eventually spreads to include everything. It is best to organize yourself, and make sure that the things get done that you have to do, while you are aware of them. If you're having trouble in this area of your life, pray for assistance.

Even if that is not the true objective behind postponing something, saying, "I will do it later," is often equivalent to "I will never do it." It's not your ex, your coworker, or fate that doesn't want you to succeed; it's your habit of procrastination. In addition to stealing your time, procrastination also steals your success, health, and future. If you continue to put off going to the gym and eating healthily, you will also delay starting your own business, attending school, or writing that book until "later," which never seems to come.

If you don't file for divorce from procrastination today, it will remain with you forever and prevent you from succeeding. Success and procrastination are incompatible concepts. There is no success where there is procrastination. Bill Gates wouldn't be a billionaire today if he had procrastinated with Microsoft. Start working on your multimillion-dollar idea right away, rather than procrastinating.

Fear of Failure

> For a righteous man may fall seven times And rise again, But the wicked shall fall by calamity. (Proverbs 24:16)

Failure is a natural part of life. Sometimes, taking a chance means failing. In actuality, the only way to guarantee success is to never attempt it, which is no way to live at all. Failure and the fear of failure are emotions that we all have felt, but if we let this fear rule us, we might never become the people God intends for us to be. Our lives will become a desolate wasteland, even though it had so much potential, when we play things safe. Failure is commonplace and not a big deal. It is an inherent aspect of life.

We all fall down in different ways. (James 3:2)

We all fall short. In actuality, failure teaches us the most about life. Failure is not fatal or conclusive. In fact, fear of failure is frequently more terrifying than the actual experience. A righteous man "falls seven times, and rises again," according to Proverbs 24:16. Even the righteous man stumbles seven times before rising. It's fine; he simply gets back up.

You are not prepared to succeed if you are afraid to fail. Failure is not a barrier to success; rather, it is a stepping stone. If you keep trying despite failure, your chances of succeeding increase. Failure is a teacher because it shows you what didn't work; if you let it, failure will inspire you to find alternative solutions that will work.

People who are unsuccessful allow failure to stifle them. In the face of failure, they give up and become inactive. You must get over your fear of failing if you want to succeed. People who are paralyzed by fear may have a brilliant concept for a project, but they frequently don't start it because they are worried that it won't succeed. What if it succeeds? Don't feel frightened by the voice of dread and failure inside of you. Giving up is the final step; failure is not! Be persistent.

Ignorance

My people are destroyed for lack of knowledge. Because you have rejected knowledge, I also will reject you from being priest for Me; Because you have forgotten the law of your God, I also will forget your children. (Hosea 4:6)

The world is continuously changing, if you refuse to learn, you will become outdated. Knowledge is power. Learning doesn't end in school. Whatever field you are in, update yourself with new information constantly. Successful people have a habit of learning. Don't convince yourself that success will soon come if you keep failing at something. No! Ask yourself honestly if you haven't caused your own failures by being ignorant. A lack of knowledge about coffee will prevent you from opening a successful coffee shop, no matter how determined and persistent you are.

If you approach your goals with ignorance, you will inevitably experience failure and defeat. Spend some time learning first. Ninety percent of your time should be devoted to learning about whatever you want to pursue. Do not do anything without first learning, and do not go into a business you do not fully understand.

Lack of Courage

Courage is not the absence of fear but the ability to take action, regardless of the circumstances. To be successful, you need to have the courage to bring your dream to reality, in spite of obstacles. The ability to make judgments in the face of adversity shows courage. Courage means taking a risk while maintaining faith in the outcome, no matter what. Although there always will be excuses for why something cannot be done, courageous people see possibilities and devise solutions. They refuse to let intimidation and fear control their choices and behaviors. They focus on getting results.

Fault-Finding

It's acceptable to recognize the error, but if you want to succeed, don't stop there. Find out how something can be fixed rather than whining about what is wrong with it. Solvers are those who achieve success. They create an umbrella rather than lament the rain.

Lack of Confidence

"If God wanted us to fly, he would have made us with wings," their father responded when the Wright brothers told him about their decision to build the plane.

Engineers were informed that building the Hoover Dam would be impossible due to its height and the difficulty of controlling that amount of water. "You are crazy; you shouldn't even undertake such a task," they were told.

More than half of Americans felt that scientists were insane when they decided to travel to the moon. Newspaper articles described how unlikely it would be for anyone to travel to the moon. The scientists were criticized by other scientists for holding such absurd beliefs and were told why it would be impossible.

Despite their lack of confidence, the Wright brothers continued their work. Today, everyone can fly around the globe with joy.

The doubters saw the Hoover Dam in person.

It was televised for everyone to see when men first set foot on the moon.

To believe in oneself is all that is necessary. Don't let others minimize your goals or declare them impractical. All you need is the belief that you can succeed. Which dream do you currently have? Who is telling you that it is not possible? Do it now, and disprove everyone else.

The Laziness Habit

It's just as bad to do the right thing as it is to do the wrong thing. Jesus related a parable about a wealthy businessman who delegated the management of enormous quantities of money to three employees while he was away. Each employee was given a certain amount of money, based on his abilities. One individual received nearly $2.5 million, another received $1 million, and a third received roughly $500,000 from the other two men. The boss cleared accounts with each employee when he got back from his trip. The boss said to the two employees that had increased their earnings, "Well done, good and faithful servant; you were faithful over a few things, and I will appoint you ruler over many things" (Matthew 25:21, 23).

However, the third worker experienced neither a profit nor a loss. When his employer came back, this man pulled up the money that he had buried. His boss was not impressed. He referred to the worker as "wicked and lazy" and gave one of his other workers the money (Matthew 25:26–28).

The purpose of the above story is not to concentrate on the various sums provided to each of the employees. Even the underperforming worker was given a tremendous amount of money to manage while his boss was away. The only thing that mattered to the employer was how each employee handled the task assigned to him. He praised his two "good and faithful" workers equally for their gains, despite the fact that they each received significantly different sums of money. He labeled the third employee as "wicked and lazy" because of his lack of effort—he didn't even put his money in a bank to earn interest.

This story serves as an example of our duty to handle the Lord's business while He is away. He has given each of us varying degrees of responsibility for overseeing His affairs. He will one day make an accounting of all the resources He has given us, including our wealth, spiritual gifts, reputation, skills, health, time, and knowledge. Every resource we possess belongs to Him (1 Corinthians 6:20). As in Jesus's parable, it doesn't matter how many resources we receive; what matters is how faithful we are with what we've been given.

You're Always Late

At some point in our lives, we have all been late for something, whether for a dinner date with friends, a doctor's appointment, or a meeting. Recognize it as one of life's inevitable occurrences, and accept that it will happen. Whenever I've struggled with lateness, I often blame it on my culture – we are always late. The reality is that persistent tardiness is not acceptable, especially in a work environment. Efficiency must be one of the most valuable things in life, if time is money, and the only thing we share in common is the number of hours in a day (i.e., achieving maximum productivity with minimum wasted effort or expense).

If you are always late, it indicates that your planning and execution of tasks are not effective. Additionally, you might be wasting someone else's time and impeding his or her productivity. People who know how to maximize their time's value are the most successful in life.

You Overspend

> Precious treasure and oil are in a wise man's dwelling,
> but a foolish man devours it. (Proverbs 21: 20 ESV)

This verse demonstrates the straightforwardness of the maxim, "Spend less than you earn." In fact, I am aware of many individuals who earn six figures or more per year but don't have a bright financial future because they have chosen a luxurious lifestyle and are spending practically all of their income.

No matter how much money you make, not saving is simply irresponsible. If you constantly have cash burning a hole in your pocket, you're putting yourself in a precarious financial situation. Your financial future and long-term success depend heavily on your ability to save money and/or invest in assets. Because we live in a capitalist culture and are frequently barraged by businesses pleading with us to spend money, it might be difficult to save, but resist the urge to indulge. By recognizing the psychological triggers that lead to your overspending, you can break the habit, though it might require determination and discipline.

The Habit of Indifference

Neglecting the needs of others ignores Jesus's example. A priest and a Levite in the Good Samaritan story came across a half-dead man by the side of the road. They didn't stop because they were preoccupied with their temple responsibilities. Later, a Good Samaritan passed by, saw the man, and stopped to assist him (Luke 10:30–36). Although the priest and Levite were engaged in God's service, their acts demonstrated a lack of understanding of what that entailed. In the meantime, the Samaritan, who wasn't even permitted to enter the temple, showed the injured traveler God's love.

Serving God requires us to prioritize the needs of others before our own. In Jesus's parable, the Samaritan put his plans on hold to save the life of the injured traveler. He didn't stop there; he also let the man ride his animal before meeting the man's needs with his resources. The Samaritan paid a high personal price for his act of kindness.

Being compassionate entails showing a genuine concern for other people's needs. It demands that we share in their suffering. In the book of Matthew, Jesus is portrayed three times as having empathy for the physical needs of those around (Matthew 9:36; 14:14; 15:32).

God first revealed Himself as El Roi, the God Who Sees, to a slave woman named Hagar in Genesis 16:13–14. Serving El Roi entailed showing compassion to others. The parable of the helpless, half-dead man reminds us of how lost in sin and doomed to death humanity was prior to God's sending Jesus to serve as our deliverer—our Good Samaritan.

Take a look at what Ephesians 2:4–7 says.

> But God, who is rich in mercy, because of His great love with which He loved us, even when we were dead in trespasses, made us alive together with Christ (by grace you have been saved), and raised us together, and made us sit together in the heavenly places in Christ Jesus, that in the ages to come He might show the exceeding riches of His grace in His kindness toward us in Christ Jesus.

It is possible to become so preoccupied with carrying out the will of God that we fail to notice the suffering people all around us. But as Christians, our aim is to love people as Christ loved the church. According to Matthew 20:28, Jesus came to earth to serve, and He frequently showered the outcasts with love. If we are sincere about following in His footsteps, we will swap out our habits of being uncaring for being kind to our fellow humans.

Envious of Other People's Lives

> Let us not become conceited, provoking one another, envying one another. (Galatians 5:26)

The Word of God is very clear about envy; it is a "work of the flesh," an incredibly dangerous and destructive sin, and we need to get rid of it completely. Jealousy will make you feel all kinds of things. It will make you feel as if nothing is going right in your life and that everyone around you is somehow much better and more capable than you. Jealousy makes you want to give up when perseverance is required to succeed. You may feel less of a person than you really are as a result. Your mind evaluates everything critically in a very bad way. You question the people around you and criticize their responses and deeds.

Envy is easier to come by now than it ever has been. Our phones provide a window into everything that others have that we do not. *If only I were them, I'd be pleased*, we think. People capture their lives in just the proper manner. Social media can be a fantastic tool for connecting with people globally, but it also encourages a lot of comparisons. Because of this, those who are successful on platforms are referred to as "influencers." People are influenced by them to believe they require more.

You might feel envy in your regular life; it's not just a social media phenomenon. You could struggle to celebrate a friend's book contract because you want to achieve the same success. You may be miffed that you still rent an apartment when your relative recently purchased a home. When you contrast your life with others, your happiness suffers. Constantly comparing your life to everyone else's will make you feel that it is lacking greatly. You will end up unable to appreciate what you already have— your achievements and the aspects of your life that could make you happy.

Sin

Sinful behavior is not to be a part of believers' everyday lives. When we sin, it affects not only us but also other people. We are cut off from God through sin. Additionally, it delays God's activity in our lives and distances us from God's will.

> Put on the Lord Jesus Christ, and make no provision
> for the flesh, to fulfill its lusts. (Romans 13:14)

God has a plan and work for you to complete. Fulfilling the purposes for which God created you will provide you with tremendous happiness and fulfillment.

A man once remarked, "Finding and carrying out God's will is success in the Christian life." Sin delays God's plan for your life. Sin impedes your development. It hinders your spiritual development. It puts God's benefits on hold. Sin prevents you from fulfilling your potential.

Undoubtedly, sin is included in the list. It is the main obstacles separating people from God Because of the consequences of sin, God had to send His one and only Son. That's serious! If you want to grow spiritually, you must become more like Christ, which means you cannot continue to live in sin (1 John 1:6).

Most of the time, we (especially young Christians) hesitate to refer to sin as what it truly is: *sin*. Call a spade a spade, please. You can't avoid these hindrances until you recognize the ideas, situations, people, and behaviors that lead to compromise.

Do you conduct business with someone who thinks it's unimportant to write a second zero on a check? Perhaps your significant other, who isn't your wife or husband yet, thinks there's nothing wrong with having sex before being married. Do you recognize the warning signs, let alone avoid them? Sin has a magnetic attraction that might keep a person from achieving her life's goals. Keep clear of it.

Relying on Your Own Strength

> My flesh and my heart fail; But God is the strength of
> my heart and my portion forever. (Psalm 73:26)

Do you use your own strength? Avoid wasting your energy! Make the most of your difficulties by depending more on God's strength. In our hours of need, God gives us both physical and spiritual strength. Some Christians have received the fortitude from God to endure long periods of captivity. I once heard a testimony of God's giving a kidnapped young woman the courage to break the chains from around her and free herself. How much more can God break the chains in your life if He can break physical chains? You were rescued on the cross of Jesus Christ by the might of God. Didn't God's power enable you to be helped in the past?

Why are you hesitant?

Trust in God!

In your hour of need, you might find strength from food, television, or the internet, but that will provide only a short-term means of reducing your suffering during trying times. You require God's unending, enduring power. There are moments when you must enter the prayer room and tell God that you need Him. You must humble yourself before the Lord and ask for His power.

Our devoted Father desires us to rely completely on Him and not on ourselves.

In actuality, you cannot develop on your own. Burnout will result if you try to accomplish something on your own. Although your active involvement is essential, God nevertheless works in you to will and to act by His good pleasure (Philippians 2:13). As a result, you must develop with the help of the Holy Spirit.

Disturbances

There are many things that demand our attention on a typical day. One of the main obstacles to spiritual development is distraction. Whenever you try to pursue a relationship with God, something or someone arises that diverts your focus from the matter. This prevents you from doing well in your growth and business.

What are you tolerating in your life, business, or profession that has hindered your productivity or ability to function? Keep in mind that you become what you tolerate in both your personal and professional lives.

When we put up with something that isn't ideal, we're just tolerating it. We allow it to continue by accepting the situation. Success means different things to every one of us, but regardless of the kind of success we pursue, there are some behaviors we must never put up with because they interfere with our productivity. We have a lot of obstacles as Christians, but God has given us the capacity to prosper. We must recognize the barriers that stand in our way and develop strategies to get above them.

CHAPTER 8

STOP COMPARING YOURSELF TO OTHERS AND START LIVING YOUR BEST LIFE

Make a careful exploration of who you are and the work you have been given, and then sink yourself into that. Don't be impressed with yourself. Don't compare yourself with others. Each of you must take responsibility for doing the creative best you can with your own life.

—Galatians 6:4–5

*I*n today's society, finding contentment is difficult. We must strive to live each day with a new perspective fixed on heaven. I asked a group of Christian women about the most significant challenge in their lives. Overwhelmingly, their answers were contentment and learning to stop comparing themselves to others. Everyone struggles with contentment, but I have found that men don't always approach it as women do. As women, we assess ourselves in relation to other women in the room almost immediately. Regardless of our circumstances, however, we can learn to be content.

Instead of yearning for what others have, do you want to start experiencing more joy in your life? Continue to read to understand more about contentment in the Bible and how a squash comparison works.

As far back as Rachel and Leah in the Old Testament, there has been a problem with comparison and envy.

> Now when Rachel saw that she bore Jacob no children, Rachel envied her sister, and said to Jacob, "Give me children, or else I die!" (Genesis 30:1)

She and her sister then started the infamous contest to see who could have the most offspring, which led to the birth of Jacob's twelve sons. Thankfully, God made the best of the circumstance and used this genealogy to bring forth the Messiah. I adore how God magnifies Himself by using our failures.

We are aware of comparison when examining our positive traits, of course. The comparison of life's challenges is virtually as widespread. We compare whether we are as *excellent* as someone else, but we also compare our troubles with those of others to determine whether theirs are worse. How can we combat this comparison spirit that Satan appears to employ so effectively against us women?

Seventeen Powerful Techniques for Managing Contentment and Avoiding Comparison

I got in touch with several reputable Christian women and asked their advice on how to stop comparing and how to be content in the modern world. I appreciate every one of these women and their abilities because they each have something unique to give. Your life will undoubtedly benefit from their insight, and I'm grateful they took the time to share their ideas.

Practice Positive Self-Talk

In addition to robbing us of joy, comparisons are an outright insult to our Creator God. We are effectively saying that God made a mistake in His unique design of our characteristics when we compare ourselves to the women next to us.

I have tried to teach my girls positive self-talk through sound theology at a young age because I am aware that they have already fallen victim to the comparison game. I will have them repeat, "God formed me, and God doesn't make mistakes," numerous times before they can exit the car and walk into school. They have heard these words repeated over and over so many times that they frequently scoff at the request, but I think that deep down, this is laying a biblical foundation of truth at the bottom of their hearts as young girls.

Imagine the benefits that would spread throughout our families, businesses, and churches if mature Christian women regularly practiced saying (and believing!) this truth.

Avoid Having a "Me" Mentality

I suggest reading Philippians. Comparing yourself to others is nothing more than selfishness dressed up as something else. The entirety of Paul's letter to the Philippi church is devoted to battling the "me" mentality and pleading with them to exercise mental restraint. It is possible to train our thinking so that the first thought that enters our minds is *not* "How does that reflect on me?" but "How does God perceive this person?" This requires a significant amount of humility, but it is achievable.

Be Thankful for Everything

So many women get caught up in the comparison trap. Because we continually see everyone's "perfect" life on social media, I think it is easy to compare lives and feel envious of others. I frequently compare my life to others and wonder why I have had hardships and tragedies when everyone else seems to have it easier. Unfortunately, comparing just increases suffering and melancholy, and it in no way resolves issues. My best piece of advice on this subject is simple but frequently challenging to implement: concentrate on your blessings. I am aware that this is far easier said than done, but when I do it, the difficulties are a little bit easier to endure. Recognize that even the seemingly picture-perfect families on social media face challenges. Everybody encounters terrible situations in life. Comparison is a terrible, misleading enemy.

Apostle Paul said,

> For I consider that the sufferings of this present time are not worthy to be compared with the glory which shall be revealed in us. (Romans 8:18)

Study the Positive Side of Others.

When used as a tool for learning, comparison might be beneficial at times. Instead of viewing life as a contest, consider what good characteristics you might pick up from others that you could apply to your own life.

We actually have less time to worry about why someone else's life is more perfect than ours if we spend our days working on our jobs, caring for our homes and relationships, and working on outreach. If we take care of ourselves by getting enough sleep, eating well, exercising outside, and engaging in spiritual renewal, perhaps we would feel better about ourselves and stop exaggerating things.

Last but not least, I think that as we women develop (not *age*) and experience life, we are less likely to compare and more likely to respect and value the distinctions we observe in other women. God gave us all of our talents to utilize for Him. Glory to Him alone!

Place More Value on the Spiritual than Physical

I firmly believe that women are rarely prevented from finding contentment by a lack of resources, uncomfortable living conditions, or even unfavorable situations. These can all be very genuine obstacles to overcome, but if I had to guess what the biggest obstacle to contentment is, I would say comparison. When we judge ourselves against others, either we feel dissatisfied with who we are and how things are going for us, or we feel superior to them. Because we are envious of others, we become ungrateful and unable to recognize our own blessings. We believe that we fall short as Christians, mothers, wives, or even friends.

We tend to believe that more is better and that happiness could be ours if only we had what others have. The Bible repeatedly forewarns us against envy. A sound heart is a life to the body, but envy is rottenness to the bones, according to Proverbs 14:30.

Make a commitment to read the Bible every day. This will make it easier for you to appreciate the spiritual over the material. You'll be more concerned about heaven than anything else on earth, as a result. Your thoughts will be more filled with thankfulness than with want.

> Set your mind on things above, not on things on the earth. (Colossians 3:2)

Christians need to have a different mentality from the rest of society.

Social Media Is Not Reality

When you read through someone's flawless Facebook images, you might not realize that they are going through personal issues. You might not be evaluating yourself against the truth of the situation. You might wish you had what others have, but since we don't always open ourselves to others and exhibit that side, you can't really understand their hardships and challenges.

Learning to be comfortable with having an only child and the agony of not being able to give that child a sibling due to infertility and the expense of adoption are two challenges I've faced in the past. There were many years when scrolling through Facebook and seeing all the pictures of families welcoming a new brother into their families was difficult, even though it was wonderful for my friends. Those same friends, however, might view all of our Bahamas trip pictures, contrast their family with ours, and wish they could bring their children along as well. They are unaware that I would swap places with them if I could.

Compare Yourself to Jesus

The greatest method, in my opinion, to put an end to comparison with others is to keep your eyes fixed on Jesus. In all of our duties as women, His Word instructs us how to live. Concentrate on it, unwind, and relish your own life. Others might measure themselves against you, but as long as your priorities are on serving Jesus, it won't matter. The issues start when we adopt an earthly perspective and observe what others do or possess.

Cast your eyes upon Jesus, and look full in His glorious face; it's a song that I love. And in the presence of His splendor and grace, earthly things will seem oddly dull.

Embrace Your Uniqueness

I make an effort to remember that God, in His infinite knowledge and creativity, made us uniquely diverse from the outside world but also from other Christian women. I have to remind myself that if everyone were exactly the same, life would be monotonous! We would never see anything fresh or interesting; our homes would always look the same, and our kids would always dress the same. Everything would be completely mindless.

Consider a skill in which you excel. Think about how long you've been doing it, whether it's a fruit of the Spirit, like kindness, or something mundane, like shopping for deals. Did you pick it up quickly? I'm going to assume you didn't. Then, keep in mind that this is how everything else in life is. Do you respect a friend who put in a lot of effort to slim down?

Inform her!

Praise her.

Don't spend the rest of the day feeling sorry for yourself while secretly wanting to punch her. Let her motivate you.

Perhaps it's more along the lines of a talent that you sincerely wish you possessed but sadly do not. Recognize that your friend or acquaintance probably doesn't have the same amazing talent that you do. I think the two of you would form a fantastic combination for a project for your congregation or neighborhood. Work together!

The devil enjoys when we have self-doubt and lack confidence. After all, if we are too busy being timid, we can't advance the kingdom. Be the best version of yourself that God created, and live and love courageously!

Celebrate Others' Strengths and Be Real

Comparing myself to others was a huge issue for me when I was younger. When I'd meet another lady for the first time, I'd compare myself to her. I discovered ways to reduce or boost myself based on my comparisons, whether it was physical attractiveness, education, wedding rings, or children.

I won't claim that I've fully gotten over this. Even though I continue to battle every day to see myself as God does, I do have a few mental defenses in place. I have to first understand that comparison is self-serving. I must look past all of these details to see a real person, who likely would be offended if she learned that I was comparing the dimensions of our wedding rings. I discovered compliments, after taking into account another person's emotions. I have to exercise caution since I have a propensity to gush, which sounds like fake praise. Now I work incredibly hard to provide genuine compliments.

When comparison rears its ugly head, I have a few encouraging statements I keep on hand:

1. *I'll never be better than anyone else at anything.* I was able to perceive everyone's potential for friendship, once I came to terms with this truth.
2. *Everyone is engaged in an unknowable conflict.* Be considerate. It doesn't matter if someone lives in a home with 8,000 square feet. Don't let position and wealth frighten you. You have no idea what troubles that person is facing.
3. Be honest about your difficulties, and avoid provoking people to make comparisons.

Most of the time, I have a happy life and am genuinely content. On social media, I attempt to present my life as genuine, without disclosing anything that should be kept out of the public eye. I'll upload images of my time in the Bahamas or a fun family vacation, but I'll also show my authentic self.

Work out your own salvation with dread and trembling.
(Philippians 2:12–13)

That Bible verse is the last and most effective item that helps me avoid comparing. There is no time for comparison if everything I do is seen as an effort to please God.

Spend Time in the Bible Rather than on Social Media

If we spend more time on Facebook than in God's Word, the comparisons won't stop. We are what we believe in our hearts to be. If we immerse ourselves in the Word, it inevitably will become the benchmark against which we measure ourselves. Instead of comparing ourselves to others, we will endeavor to live up to it.

But if Facebook or Instagram becomes our major source of information, then, of course, the deluge of the veneer of idealized lives portrayed there will make us despondent when we reflect; contentment will be elusive. Therefore, I believe that we should intentionally spend time in the Bible every day. Godliness and contentment make a powerful combination.

Celebrate Who God Created You to Be

I think that accepting our God-given blessings with gratitude is the best cure for unhappiness. I find it beneficial to actively ponder that God gave me my personality, abilities, physical blessings, and position in life. I am happiest and most glorifying to God when I lean into who He made me to be, and I stop trying to be someone else. He made me who I am and put me where I am for a reason. As a result, I'm making an effort to better recognize my gifts, praise God for them, and seek His guidance on how to use them for His cause.

Additionally, I find that the internet accentuates my tendency toward comparison and unhappiness. Setting social media restrictions for myself seems to help reduce some of these temptations.

Always Focus on the Real Standard.

I pause and ask myself, "Is this the gold standard?" whenever I am tempted to compare myself to others (how much good they do, how wonderful of a mother/wife they are, etc.). I then try to concentrate on Jesus. Even though I will never be able to match His flawless example, as long as I try to model my life after Him, I am confident that I am enough. I am sufficient because of His incredible grace and deep affection. I'm not judged by the same standards as the woman sitting next to me. I am, nonetheless, held to Jesus's standards. I'm instructed to imitate Him.

It makes no difference if my house or financial account are smaller than others. I don't care if I'm not as trim, toned, attractive, or stylish as my friends. What counts is that my heart resembles that of Jesus. If I concentrate on that, I'll feel good about those women and keep trying to become more and more like Jesus.

Seek Only His Fulfillment

For a very long time, I have suffered with comparison. It's frequently about my size or my skills—mainly that since becoming a mother. Social networking was the worst for me. But also, the women I met gave the impression that they "had it all together" at a time when I felt like I was tumbling apart. After having children, I struggled with anxiety, despair, and insecurity. I frequently gave myself permission to believe that I was the only woman who struggled in the way that I did and that other women didn't struggle at all!

But God's work in me changed me. And it comes from just Him. I have spent more time with my Lord. I'm doing more reading and prayer. Instead of turning to other people, food, TV, or anything else, I am going to Him with my worries and troubles.

Every day, I fervently seek out the Holy Spirit and beg Him to assist me. I am aware that only in Him do I find fulfillment.

I will never be pleased or fulfilled if I look for satisfaction in a clean house, my job as a wife or mother, my proficiency in writing or speaking, or even my capacity to win people to Christ, as none of these things can completely fill the need left by God in my heart—just Him! As my confidence grows, I see that I'm no longer comparing myself to others as much, not from one of my own sources but by Him. I have adopted this phrase as my motto: "His grace is sufficient for me." My source of energy is now the Holy Spirit.

Focus Your Thoughts on God

A fantastic verse to read when battling with unhappiness is Philippians 4. I think that cultivating satisfaction is mostly a matter of self-control. In the end, we get to decide which thoughts we let stay in our heads. We must first feed the positive thoughts while starving the negative ones (Philippians 4:8). I simply remind myself—out loud, if necessary!—"I am not going to focus on that negative notion," whenever a sensation of unhealthy comparison or sadness over worldly circumstances enters my head. I then decide to shift my focus to something uplifting by singing a hymn or uttering a prayer of gratitude (Philippians 4:6–7).

This is a process that I occasionally go through five times in quick succession when I'm truly having trouble with a certain problem. And it's all right! All of this is done in the service of molding and enslaving every thought to follow Christ.

We must actively seek the positive aspects of every circumstance. The light of God's love and caring for us shines brightest during our darkest moments. A good chance to demonstrate for our children and experience the contentment Paul spoke of in Philippians 4:11–12 is presented by trying situations.

Finally, we must work on the kingdom's tasks! It is much

simpler to silence the voices of comparison and dissatisfaction from the outside world if I am sincerely committed to loving God, serving His church, evangelizing the lost, and caring for the family He has blessed me with.

Lay Off the Worldly Expectations

In addition to stealing joy, comparison also steals satisfaction and a virtuous lifestyle. We are employing the incorrect standard of comparison when we assess ourselves in relation to others. We ought to compare ourselves to Christ, the ideal standard. When we observe individuals around us and attempt to follow them in areas of expediency, I believe we frequently defraud ourselves and those close to us of blessings. We are instructed to put every burden aside in order to complete the Christian race (Hebrews 12:1). So let's avoid carrying around unwieldy (or materialistic) expectations that will obstruct our progress.

Comparison—it looks bad. It raises others to unattainable heights and lowers us to unattainable lows (or rare occasions, it could be the opposite). Comparison diverts our attention from what is important—the spiritual—too frequently in favor of the physical. So how do we resist this temptation every day with satisfaction?

Apostle Paul said,

> Not that I speak in regard to need, for I have learned in whatever state I am, to be content: I know how to be abased, and I know how to abound. Everywhere and in all things I have learned both to be full and to be hungry, both to abound and to suffer need. I can do all things through Christ who strengthens me. (Philippians 4:11–13)

I know how to prosper and how to be brought low. We develop satisfaction via Jesus, just like Paul did. Knowing that God is our ultimate source of sufficiency leads to contentment.

Our hearts and thoughts are so full of the goodness of the benefits we have received from above that we realize we have no time for pointless comparison in our lives.

Gain Contentment in Hardship

Comparison steals our joy. That phrase truly touched me the first time I heard it. I was a first-time mother, dealing with a sleep-deprived child (I still do). I had just spent the entire day reading on Facebook after trying unsuccessfully for hours to put my infant to sleep so I could have a meal. I saw that many of my friends had a lot of freedom with their kids, and I was immediately in a woe-is-me frame of mind. My heart dropped.

Before this point in my life, I don't recall how many sermons about contentment I had listened to and nodded yes to. How often did I think, *Of course I am always happy?* Alternatively, I'd think, *I wouldn't let that get to me! I don't care about the huge house or expensive car enough to be unhappy.*

Well, to my surprise, there are numerous ways to be content. For the sake of Christ, then, I am content with weaknesses, insults, sufferings, persecutions, and disasters (2 Corinthians 12:10) because I am stronger when I am weak. Why was I allowing the joy that had been given to me to be diminished by my "difficulty"—a beautiful hardship, I should add. God instructs us to be content in numerous verses of His Word, in *all* things, regardless of the situation—content. As Christian women, let's be shining examples of contentment in all ways.

Do Not Attempt to Do It All

In the modern world, contentment is a difficult quality to nurture. Paul claims to have acquired the ability to be content in every circumstance (Philippians 4). How can we, as Christian women, accomplish that? To find contentment in all circumstances, we must spend time in the Bible, pray, and work every day. Limiting our time on social media is one useful strategy for doing that.

We might easily feel disheartened or unsatisfied with our families, our houses, or our possessions in today's "Pinterest perfect" environment. We frequently feel unsatisfied as a result of posts or images we've viewed on social media. We experience pressure to throw extravagant birthday parties for our children. We feel under pressure to maintain tidy, perfectly furnished homes. We experience pressure to travel lavishly, document every moment, and publish about it online. We experience pressure to possess the ideal physique. The amount of time we spend on social media will decrease if we set time limits. Yes, there will still be occasions when we compare our homes or families to someone else's, but we can only hope that these moments are fleeting and do not distract us from living in God's purpose for us.

CHAPTER 9

PERSEVERING THROUGH SETBACK

My brethren, count it all joy when you fall into various trials, knowing that the testing of your faith produces patience. But let patience have its perfect work, that you may be perfect and complete, lacking nothing.

—James 1:2–4

*N*obody achieves success or fulfills purpose without experiencing at least one significant setback. The life of believers is not a deadline to glory, but they certainly get there. The life of the believer is not like the highway through Nebraska but like a state highway through the Blue Ridge Mountains of Tennessee. There are scenes and chasms, dark wisps of mist, bears, and slippery and hairpin bends. Yet on this perilous winding road, where you cannot see far ahead, signs are frequently erected that proclaim, "The best is yet to come." And at the bottom right corner of the sign, in someone's handwriting, are the words: "As I live, says the Lord!"

The story of Ruth shows us that even if life's journey is filled with obstacles, a Christian will eventually achieve unspeakable joy. The Bible is open and honest about pain. Life is hardly a calm ride; it's an arduous journey. You occasionally see that the rubber of your life is wearing off. Some setbacks—illness, depression, financial difficulties, marital issues, or losing a loved one—are so severe that you are unsure of your ability to continue. But the book of Ruth is like a large sign that directs you to continue in this direction as a woman in Christ. Paradise is ahead. It teaches you that God's invisible hand has mapped out your path, and He is not guiding you down a cliff. The book of Ruth gives hope in the midst of setbacks.

God is guiding you toward honor and a second chance. The book of Ruth is one of those signs that we are to read, especially as Christian women. Its message is one of encouragement and hope. It is a reminder that all of the setbacks in our lives are not dead ends but that God is at work to create joy for us.

The story of Ruth reads like a series of setbacks. In chapter 1, Naomi and her two sons had to leave their homeland in Judah because of a famine. Then Naomi's husband died. Their sons marry Moabite women, and for ten years, the women seem barren. Then her sons die, and Naomi is at home with her two sons' widows. Although Ruth clings to her, chapter 1 closes with Naomi's bitter lamentation: "I went full, and the Lord brought me back empty ... The Almighty hath done me evil."

In chapter 2, Naomi regains hope when Boaz appears on the scene as a possible candidate to marry Ruth. But he does not propose marriage to Ruth. He takes no steps at all. At least that's how it seems initially. The chapter ends in overflowing hope, in great suspense, and in uncertainty as to how everything will work out.

In chapter 3, Naomi and Ruth risk a daring midnight adventure. Ruth goes to Boaz on the threshing floor and says, in effect, "I want you to spread your wings over me as my husband." But just as the tragedy of Ruth's widowhood seems to unwind into a beautiful love story, the rock of the Blue Ridge Mountains falls onto the road in Ruth's life. According to Hebrew custom, there is one who takes precedence over taking Ruth as a wife. Blameless and sincere as he is, Boaz will not take a step until the law is satisfied. So the third chapter closes in anticipation of another setback.

> Now Boaz went up to the gate and sat down there; and behold, the close relative of whom Boaz had spoken came by. So Boaz said, "Come aside, friend, sit down here." So he came aside and sat down. And he took ten men of the elders of the city, and said, "Sit down here." So they sat down. Then he said to the close relative, "Naomi, who has come back from the country of Moab, sold the piece of land which belonged to our brother Elimelech. And I thought to inform you, saying, 'Buy it back in the presence of the inhabitants and the elders of my people. If you will redeem it, redeem it; but if you will not redeem it, then tell me, that I may know; for there is no one but you to redeem it, and I am next after you.'" And he said, "I will redeem it." Then Boaz said, "On the day you buy the field from the hand of Naomi, you must also buy it from Ruth the Moabitess, the wife of the dead, to perpetuate the name of the dead through his inheritance." And the close relative said, "I cannot redeem it for myself, lest I ruin my own inheritance. You redeem my right of redemption for yourself, for I cannot redeem it." Now this was the custom in former times in Israel concerning redeeming and exchanging, to confirm anything: one man took off his sandal and gave it to the other, and this was a confirmation in Israel. Therefore the close relative said to Boaz, "Buy it for yourself." So he took off his sandal. And Boaz said to the elders and all the people, "You are witnesses this day that I have bought all that was Elimelech's, and all that was Chilion's and Mahlon's, from the hand

of Naomi. Moreover, Ruth the Moabitess, the widow of Mahlon, I have acquired as my wife, to perpetuate the name of the dead through his inheritance, that the name of the dead may not be cut off from among his brethren and from his position at the gate. You are witnesses this day."

And all the people who were at the gate, and the elders, said, "We are witnesses. The Lord make the woman who is coming to your house like Rachel and Leah, the two who built the house of Israel; and may you prosper in Ephrathah and be famous in Bethlehem. May your house be like the house of Perez, whom Tamar bore to Judah, because of the offspring which the Lord will give you from this young woman." So Boaz took Ruth and she became his wife; and when he went in to her, the Lord gave her conception, and she bore a son. Then the women said to Naomi, "Blessed be the Lord, who has not left you this day without a close relative; and may his name be famous in Israel! And may he be to you a restorer of life and a nourisher of your old age; for your daughter-in-law, who loves you, who is better to you than seven sons, has borne him." Then Naomi took the child and laid him on her bosom, and became a nurse to him. Also the neighbor women gave him a name, saying, "There is a son born to Naomi." And they called his name Obed. He is the father of Jesse, the father of David.

Now this is the genealogy of Perez: Perez begot Hezron; Hezron begot Ram, and Ram begot Amminadab; Amminadab begot Nahshon, and Nahshon begot Salmon; Salmon begot Boaz, and Boaz begot Obed; Obed begot Jesse, and Jesse begot David. (Ruth 4:1–22)

More Setbacks on the Road to Glory

After the midnight scene in Chapter 3, Boaz goes to the city gate, where public business is conducted. The closer relative comes by, and Boaz explains the situation to him. Naomi gives up what little property she has; the closer relative has the obligation to buy the property so that the inheritance stays in the family. At the end of the fourth verse, he says to our grief, "I will solve it." But we don't want that. We want Boaz to solve it. There seems to be another setback. The irony is that this setback is due to justice. The fellow is only doing his duty.

Sometimes, the federal highway in the Blue Ridge Mountains is totally clogged, not necessarily with boulders or bears, but with good workers just doing their duty.

When we want to say, "No, stop! Don't let that other fellow take Ruth," Boaz says to the near relative, "You know that Naomi has a daughter-in-law. If you fulfill Your Redeemer duty, do you have to marry her [Ruth] and raise descendants for her [deceased] husband Mahlon?"

To our great relief, in Ruth 3:6, the relative says he cannot do it. Maybe he's already married. Whatever the case, we rejoice in the background as Boaz comes through that gorge in the Blue Ridge and heads straight for the wedding reception with beautiful young Ruth on his arm.

But the clouds are gathering. Ruth is barren—at least, it seems so. In Ruth 1:4, we learn that no children came of the ten-year marriage with Mahlon.

The tension never ends.

Do you understand how we can learn from the book of Ruth that the life of believers is not a straight line to glory? Life is made up of many bends. We don't know what's to come. The main idea of the story is that the best is yet to come. If you love God, the best is yet to come, no matter where you are.

Why Is Naomi the Focus?

The clouds that afflict Ruth and Boaz abound in grace and pour down upon their heads in streams of blessing (quoted from the hymn "God Moves in a Mysterious Way" by William Cowper) in Chapter 4:13:

> So Boaz took Ruth, and she became his wife and he came in to her. And the Lord gave her conception, and she gave birth to a son.

But notice that in Ruth 4:14–17, the focus is not on Ruth at all or on Boaz. The focus is on Naomi and the child.

Why?

Before I answer this question, I am reminded of an encounter. A few years ago, a scruffy-looking person came to the church's monthly food giveaway. I asked him what his name was, and he said, "Difficult times, that's my name. Difficult times."

Well, at the beginning of Ruth, Naomi's name was "Hard Times"—Hard Times Naomi. The lesson of this book is that the life of believers is not a straight line to glory, but they will certainly get there.

The story began with Naomi's loss. It ended with Naomi's win. It began with death and ended with birth. A son—for whom? In Ruth 4:17, we see the great goal in Naomi's long, winding path.

> And the neighbor women gave him a name, saying, "A son is born to Naomi!"

Not to Ruth but to Naomi! Why? To show that what Naomi said in Ruth 1:21 was not true—"the Lord brought her back empty from Moab."

If only we could learn to wait and trust God, then all our complaints against God would prove untrue.

Signposts of God's Gracious Action in Bitter Setbacks

Ruth was written to help us recognize the signposts of God's grace in our lives and to trust in His grace, even when the clouds are so dark that we no longer see the way, much less the signposts on the side. Let us look back and realize that God was at work, turning every setback into a stepping stone to joy. It is God who plans well in all our bitter fortunes.

God set Ruth at Naomi's side when her life was about to sink in Moab. We see this in two verses. In Ruth 1:16, we learn that Ruth's bond with Naomi is based on the bond with Naomi's God—"Your God is my God." God had won Ruth's faithfulness in Moab, so Naomi owed to God the amazing love of her daughter-in-law.

Ruth 2:12 also says that when Ruth came to Judah with Naomi, she took refuge under God's wing. Therefore, it is thanks to God that Ruth left her home and family to follow and care for Naomi. All along, God was turning Naomi's setbacks into joy, even when she was unaware of His mercy.

Boaz's Perseverance

In Ruth 1, Naomi gives the impression that Ruth is hopeless in marrying again and raising children to carry on the family name (1:12). In the meantime, however, God kept a wealthy, godly man named Boaz to do just that. In Ruth 2:20, Naomi herself admits that God is at work. She recognizes that behind the "accidental" meeting of Ruth and Boaz hides the grace of God, which He has not withdrawn from either the living or the dead. In every loss that befalls believers, God is already at work for their gain.

Who was it that gave birth to a child to Ruth after her barrenness so that the women of the neighborhood could say, "A son was born to Naomi"? God gave the child. Look at Ruth 4:11; the townspeople pray for Boaz and Ruth. Ruth was childless after ten years of marriage. They remembered Rachel, whose bosom the Lord opened long ago. And they prayed that God would make Ruth like Rachel and Leah.

The writer makes it very clear in Ruth 4:13 who was responsible for the conception of the child.

> Boaz took her, and the Lord caused her to become pregnant.

We repeatedly observe that God was at work in Naomi's heartbreaking setbacks. God granted Ruth to Naomi after she lost her husband and sons. When she could not think of a relative who could raise descendants for the family name, God gave her Boaz. When Ruth, who was barren, married Boaz, God gave birth to a child. In the life of Naomi, we see the point of the story. The lives of believers are not in a straight line to glory, but God sees that they get there.

Is *Glory* Too Strong a Word?

Perhaps the town's people felt that the word *glory* was a bit of an exaggeration. After all, it's only a child—a grandmother holding a child after a long, hard, heartbreaking life. Ah, but that's not the end of the story.

If the story of Ruth in the small Judean village ended with an old grandmother holding her new grandchild, then glory would be too big a word. But the author doesn't stop there. He lifts up his eyes to the forests and the snowy peaks of salvation history. In Ruth 4:17, he is simply saying that this child, Obed, is the father of Jesse, and Jesse is the father of David.

Suddenly, we realize that something has been brewing here that is beyond our imagination. God didn't just plan a temporary blessing for a few Jews in Bethlehem. He prepared the coming of the greatest king Israel ever had, David. And in the name of David is united the hope of the Messiah, of the new age, of peace, of justice, and of freedom from pain, tears, sorrow, and guilt. This simple little story leads to the great river of hope.

God's Glorious Action through History

The book of Ruth teaches us that God's plan for His own is to connect us to something much greater than ourselves. God wants us to understand, as we follow Him, that our lives are always more meaningful than we realize. For Christians, there is always a connection between the ordinary occurrences of everyday life and the mighty acts of God in history. Anything done in the slightest obedience to God is meaningful. It is part of the cosmic mosaic that God is fashioning to manifest His great power and wisdom to the world and to the authorities and authorities in heaven (Ephesians 3:10).

The deep fulfillment of a Christian's life is that it is not ruled by trifles. Serving a widowed mother-in-law, gleaning grain, finding love, having a baby—for the Christian, all these things are connected with eternity. You are part of something much bigger than meets the eye.

The word *glory* is not too strong. The lives of believers are not in a straight line to glory, but they will certainly get there. God is watching. There is a hope that goes far beyond the cute baby and the happy grandmother. If it were not so, we would be the most miserable people of all. The story points to David. David continues to point to Jesus. And Jesus goes on to point to the resurrection of our perishable bodies (Romans 8:23), when "there will be no more death, nor mourning, nor outcry, nor pain: for the first things have passed" (Revelation 21:4).

The best is yet to come. This unshakable truth is manifested in the lives of men and women who follow Christ in the obedience of faith. I say it to the young, who are strong and full of hope, and to the old, whose outer shells are slowly withering. The best is yet to come.

Setback for a Purpose from a Joseph Story

> As for you, you meant evil against me, but God meant
> it for good, to bring it about that many people[a] should
> be kept alive, as they are today. (Genesis 50:20 ESV)

Let's look at an example from the life of Joseph. God frequently uses setbacks to advance us. As we reflect on these words, let's ponder how frequently we have experienced this truth in our own lives. Many times, what first appears to be a devastating setback ends up being an advancement from God.

When Joseph's brothers sold him, the youngest son of Jacob, into slavery in Egypt, he must have felt let down. Jacob's favorite son was Joseph. God offered him mind-blowing discoveries through dreams when he was a young man. In one, he imagined himself exalted above his parents and his eleven brothers. As a result of Joseph talking to his brothers about his dreams, eventually they came to the conclusion that Joseph had to go.

The brothers devised a scheme to sell Joseph into slavery, and Joseph soon found himself behind bars. It took thirteen years before Joseph was given the chance to interpret one of Pharaoh's dreams. Joseph won Pharaoh's admiration to the point where Pharaoh appointed Joseph to be the ruler of all of Egypt as his right-hand man.

In Joseph's darkest hours, when everything in his life seemed to be going against God's plan, Joseph discovered his trust in the Lord. He was propelled forward for a divine purpose at God's time. Joseph not only prevented the hunger of his own family and the people of Israel but also of all of Egypt.

The amazing words of forgiveness that Joseph was later able to speak to his brothers as an elderly man were, "Don't be afraid. God intended good when you meant harm."

The Lord had changed the bad aim of his brothers into something good. It was not possible to exact personal retribution.

Joseph had come to see that the act that was intended to bring about his demise had served God's good purpose.

Give Yourself over to God's Plan

Remember Joseph and Naomi if you're feeling disappointed by an apparent detour. Even when your intentions were changed, God can still be orchestrating something surprisingly good. Now could be a good time to review the following promises found in the Bible:

> My brethren, count it all joy when you fall into various trials, knowing that the testing of your faith produces patience. But let patience have its perfect work, that you may be perfect and complete, lacking nothing. (James 1:2–4)

> And we know that all things work together for good to those who love God, to those who are the called according to His purpose. (Romans 8:28)

Before we start learning to trust God for a successful outcome in the Christian life, it frequently takes a few disappointments and diversions. Let Joseph's and Naomi's stories serve as motivation for what God can accomplish when you submit to His will in the face of anger and failure. When Jesus said, "Whoever wants to be my disciple must deny themselves and take up their cross and follow me," He meant exactly what you read.

> For whoever desires to save his life will lose it, but whoever loses his life for My sake will find it. (Matthew 16:25)

First, it could seem frightening. Giving up control is difficult, but you must do so if you want the Holy Spirit to be able to use your power to accomplish His mission through you. Jesus had experience with giving up. He followed His Father's instructions to the letter. He was able to sacrifice His life on the cross for us because of this. Jesus urges us to follow Him, to pick up our crosses and completely submit to God.

The best time to let go and trust God is when everything falls apart and you don't comprehend God's purpose. Have faith that He will lead you to an unexpected turn for your benefit.

Gratitude to God, Even in a Setback

> And we know that all things work together for good to those who love God, to those who are the called according to His purpose. Romans 8:28

Setbacks typically are seen negatively, yet the Bible says that as believers, everything works out for our best interests. Be aware that this verse reads "all things work together for good," *not* "all things are good." In other words, no matter how horrible or negative a situation may seem, it always works out for your benefit in the end.

Setbacks often have an unnoticed benefit. A setback may position you to rise above your circumstances and never fall and lead you to the place of purpose. Although God is not the cause of failures, He can use them to propel you into a position where you will be encouraged and promoted. Have you ever had a setback in any area of your life? Instead of living in regret or feeling sorry for yourself, it's time for you to express gratitude and praise to God, and you'll see how He uses it to your advantage. God be praised!

CHAPTER 10

FULFILLING YOUR PURPOSE

I cry out to God Most High, to God who will fulfill his purpose for me. (Psalm 57:2 NLT)

Your eyes saw my unformed body; all the days ordained for me were written in your book before one of them came to be. (Psalm 139:16)

*H*ave you ever given these verses serious thought? It is amazing to think that God is aware of every day of your life. It can be both comforting and overwhelming. Knowing your purpose is one thing, but fulfilling your life's purpose is another. As we become older, it becomes more difficult to see this in terms of destiny. Your destiny lies in discovering and fulfilling your purpose. A woman's purpose is not limited to marriage or bearing children. Some people go above and beyond to do the work God called them to accomplish. When you know your purpose, you will achieve it with little thought of monetary benefits, although it is important to make a living with your purpose.

In the midst of your hectic life, it is crucial to ask yourself, "What am I destined for?" You ask the God in whom you have faith to help you discover what your purpose is in life so that you can use it to make a difference. When you go to bed at night and you endure sleepless nights, you must be able to say, "This is what I'm here for, and this is how I will go about it." It need not be grand or impressive or even bring you money.

Have you ever awakened in a pitch-black space with no light at all? Did you accomplish anything productive? Living a life without a defined purpose is like that. Beloved, God wants you to serve as an example of how He lived on earth. This is one of the main reasons He allowed you to remain on this planet after you surrendered your heart to Christ. He asked you to serve as His change ambassador, and He wants you to fulfill a life goal.

Apostle Paul said,

> Brethren, I do not count myself to have apprehended; but one thing I do, forgetting those things which are behind and reaching forward to those things which are ahead, I press toward the goal for the prize of the upward call of God in Christ Jesus. (Philippians 3:13–14)

We can see that Paul's having a clear understanding of what God wanted him to do was one of the things that helped him achieve his goal. He never lacked confidence. He was completely aware of both his calling and with whom he was to work. He was aware that his task was to share the good news of our Lord Jesus Christ with the Gentiles. Paul dedicated himself to fulfilling his calling and accomplished much for the kingdom.

Do you realize that God also has called you to a life of purpose? You weren't just one of the many that Jesus saved. No, He redeemed you and exalted you to a glorious life. He saved you so that you may have a significant impact on the world for His kingdom. But you have to do it on purpose. In order to take advantage of what God has in store for you, you must set aside part of your time to realign yourself. God wants you to significantly advance and move into a greater dimension of His plan and purpose for your life as woman.

God has chosen your life's purpose. It cannot be negotiated. God's purpose for your life cannot be changed; this is analogous to saying that water is wet. Even if you might not be serving the reason for which you were created, God still has a plan for you. This is God's design for you. He sent Jesus to the earth for a reason, and He has a reason for your life.

This does not imply that there is one very specific niche available for you to fill and that it will be your fault if you don't get it. I believe there are numerous, inventive ways for you to accomplish your goals. The pressure should decrease as a result. If you choose the inappropriate college, job, or mate, you won't completely alter the trajectory of your life. God is far more powerful than any error in judgment or disobedience on your side.

> The Lord will accomplish his plan for me. (Psalm 138:8)

By defining your purpose, you may decide in which activities you should engage. You shouldn't engage in activities that go against God's plan for your life, just like Jesus did. Jesus's mission was to carry out the Father's wishes and serve as the world's Savior. Jesus only acted when His Father directed Him. Because of their close relationship, Jesus was able to perceive what the Father was doing.

Your Passion and Purpose Must Be Fulfilled

In order to fulfill your passion and purpose, you must make a conscious decision to step into the light of God's directive for you. By stepping into the light, you are expressing your readiness and willingness to share who you really are and of what you are capable with the rest of the world. It indicates that you want the world to know about your talents and the impact you hope to have on people's lives.

Additionally, stepping into the light indicates that you have arrived at a stage in life where your only concern is achieving your goals and engaging in activities that bring you complete fulfillment.

You must do some actions, however, to assist you in holding on and remaining focused on the objective before you can disclose yourself to the world. These actions will assist you in sustaining your interest after the initial few weeks or months. Note that the dream that comes true without effort is not a dream.

1. **Prepare your mind**. Simple, right? It is common practice to mentally prepare yourself before deciding. It's a determination to keep going even when it seems like you are not progressing; it's a decision to continually stay focused on achieving your mission and not give up, despite any obstacles you could encounter. You must get ready mentally because the initial stages of pursuing your passion might not be encouraging. The following are some likely scenarios that you might experience:
   - Nobody will listen to you in the beginning.
   - Nobody instantly identifies you.
   - Nobody can be persuaded to listen to you later.

   It is crucial to mentally prepare for these scenarios because they will make you feel completely alone. If you adhere to the following step, you might not feel entirely alone.

2. **Talk to a positive-minded friend**. Having supportive and like-minded individuals nearby is important when you take a conscious action to live out your passion and purpose because you need them to motivate you when things don't go as planned.

It's not necessary to surround yourself with a lot of people; one or two reliable friends, a mentor, or someone who shares your passions and objectives is sufficient. It is best to have someone who will assist you in getting up under your own initiative. You are not alone if you have such a person in your life.

People are inspired to learn more about your interest when they witness your friend or mentor supporting you. You attract more engagement and interest in your passion, thanks to their support and encouragement.

3. **Conduct research**. If you want to find something, there's nothing better than researching. The simple fact is that your passion and purpose are shared by someone else. Others had it before you, and others will have it after you. Do your homework to learn the steps that people who came before you took to achieve their success. Say, for instance, that public speaking on career growth is an area you love. You might not be able to write about this passion, but you likely can speak passionately about it.

Speaking and writing are two distinct skills; some people may be able to accomplish both, while others only possess one of these abilities. You can only write about career advancement; or you can only speak about it.

Why not research what the experts in your sector are doing to gain recognition?

Here's a thought: why not record a brief video of yourself speaking enthusiastically about your chosen topic—say, career development—for at least five minutes? Appearing in front of a camera obviously constitutes public speaking.

Why not write out what you said in your short video? You need to write something compelling to get people to click on it in order to persuade them to view your short video. By doing this, you are developing yourself and improving your communication, writing, and other skills related to your passion. You must, however, take this next step in order to remain consistent and gain recognition for your brief videos.

4. **Create your platform.** I stated earlier that choosing to live out your passion and purpose requires stepping into the spotlight. In order to draw attention to what you do best and gain recognition for it, personal branding is crucial. By positioning yourself as an authority in your field and enhancing your credibility, you can advance your passion as a career, widen your circle of influence, and have a bigger impact. Personal branding is a conscious and deliberate effort to create and influence public perception of you. Therefore, create a platform that works well for you, and develop your brand in order to gain awareness.

    Consider the preceding example—say you enjoy speaking publicly about career growth. YouTube could be a platform you use to develop your brand. Facebook and LinkedIn are additional social media sites to use. The aim is to create a brief description of your video that will ultimately entice your target audience to click on the link to your YouTube video. Even if YouTube is your primary platform, you can also use the other social media sites to drive visitors to your channel and develop your brand. By doing this, people will regard you as a leader in your field.

5. **Have focus and consistency.** Establishing your authority in your industry needs a steady and consistent process that calls for you to never give up, even when the going gets tough and progress seems slow. Consistency is key to brand development. Ask a mason; he doesn't stop until the project is finished. You must continue to develop if you want to have impact. There is no end because you affect people's lives and have an influence every day. You fulfill

a purpose each day. Fulfilling your passion and purpose is the aim.

6. **Pray**. Prayer is a crucial action if you are a believer. At the end of the day, you will realize that you can't handle everything on your own. Why worry when you can pray? You will come to the realization that you require inner fortitude to keep you afloat. Why stress if things are moving slowly when you can simply pray about everything and trust that your prayers are heard? This has major significance. Believe that it has been resolved and that everything is in order. At the end of the day, everything will fall into place if you maintain your hope and trust.

You will be well on your way to accomplishing better things if you put these six steps into practice. Your enthusiasm will be visible to everyone. You merely need to continue being consistent and demonstrating your abilities to everyone.

I developed these stages based on my own experience. I intentionally took these actions in order to have a significant impact and to be a powerful figure in my industry.

These are the same steps I took to develop my purpose as a woman who is fervently committed to progress, self-improvement, passion, and purpose. I put these instructions together in an effort to help you as much as the steps have helped me. Having a determined intention to make your voice heard via focus and consistency can help you to navigate the challenging beginning effortlessly.

Things That Prevent You from Fulfilling Your God-Given Purpose

It's fascinating to see how other people find and carry out their God-given purposes. You might be left wondering when it will be your chance to live the life of your dreams because others are living it. When you examine your life, you might be unable to identify what prevents you from achieving your goal.

In Chapter 7, I mentioned some hindrances that maybe preventing you from living God's purpose for you. You are aware of the purpose that God has given you, yet there are obstacles in your way—many of which you cannot see. You might become discouraged and inclined to withdraw and stick with what you know.

You are not alone.

The Israelites were dissatisfied when Moses took a long time to return after ascending Mount Sinai. When the promised land seemed like a far-off dream that would never be realized, they wanted to pack up and head back to Egypt. Although they didn't return, their hearts did.

Avoid giving in to the need to change your mind because of factors that prevent you from carrying out your God-given mission. Ask God to reveal these things to you and how to get through them.

No matter what challenges you encounter, your mission is unique from others; it is essential and has the power to change your life.

Consider the following most frequent challenges that prevent you from achieving your God-given assignment:

1. Distraction or Worry

A distraction is something that diverts your focus from another task; you are drawn away from the main point. Distractions simply slow you down and cause you to lose focus when your mission calls for complete focus. They're not awful things, but you don't consider them as important.

Worry is one of the key factors that can divert you from your goal. When you desire to fulfill God's plan for your life, your mind is preoccupied with questions, like how you'll make money, how you'll pay your bills, what other people will say, and so on. This can get your thoughts off of the work that God has called you to undertake and keep them on the wrong things. You may spend a lot of time considering how you can become more like your social media siblings when you contrast your purpose path with theirs. You may experience feelings of inadequacy and self-doubt, which can cause you to procrastinate on your work.

It's possible to endure a financial slump when switching from a job to your purpose work, and you may succumb to the pressure to start a side business. This will slow you down and cause you to lose focus on what God is asking you to do. Additionally, if you focus too much on earning money, your God-given destiny may get put off.

You may feel lonely on your purpose quest and be tempted to find solace in television shows, movies, or YouTube videos. After seeing one film or episode, you're eager to see more. Time passes as you are watching, and you start to lose focus. After binge-watching, working might occasionally be unpleasant. Your appetite for entertainment begs you to satisfy it.

Avoid acting or carrying out tasks that God has not given you. He has vowed to meet your necessities while you carry out His task. Pray to God for wisdom in place of worrying. The Word of God should take up a sizable portion of your leisure time.

2. Wrong Partnerships

Forging alliances is essential to achieving your God-given mission. The ideal candidates have a strong network of support and place high importance on purpose and vision. People who are aware of your calling from God and who can hold you accountable when you stray from it make up a strong alliance. Making the wrong partnerships can drain your mental, emotional, and spiritual energy. Such people also will take you in the wrong direction. How, then, do you locate the ideal alliance for your needs?

> The Lord says, "Woe to the rebellious children, who take counsel, but not of Me, And who devise plans, but not of My Spirit, That they may add sin to sin." (Isaiah 30:1)

You can build a godly alliance with the proper people, thanks to the guidance of the Holy Spirit. You will be drawn to the people with whom God wants you to stand at this time. Some alliances are short-lived, while others last a lifetime. Discover how to tell them apart. Making the wrong alliance can jeopardize your future. Alliances can be created with close friends, coworkers, groups, or anyone with whom you engage frequently.

You occasionally will part ways with those in your relationships; they supported you in the past but now are holding you back. Do you have a friend with whom you've disclosed personal information about your goals, but she continues to encourage you to pursue other opportunities? That advice will make you go backward rather than forward. It's time to let go of such relationships. Keep in touch with people who support you from the heart.

3. Lack of Enthusiasm

Your God-given destiny is fueled by passion. Even if some portions of your mission might not be enjoyable, your passion will help you persevere. Persecution, rejection, desertion, betrayal, and an unending list of other negative experiences await those who choose to follow Christ and live out His plan for their lives. When you fall in love with God's work, you will persevere through difficulties and resist the urge to give up. People who labor for God will admit that sometimes the going is rough, and they want to close up shop and go home. The fire continues to burn, however, because of the power of God at work in them and other people.

Think about what would have happened if Paul had given up preaching the gospel due to shipwrecks, assaults, robbers, false believers, and so on. Paul persisted until the very end because he genuinely was committed to seeing the Gentiles come to know Jesus Christ.

Many obstacles in life may test your faith and cause you to lose interest in doing God's will. You might question whether it is worthwhile to seek God's aspirations for your life when your most prized dreams crumble in front of your eyes.

God is the only one who can restore your purpose's lost enthusiasm. Jesus declared that you will produce a lot of fruit when you abide in Him and He in you. Keep your relationship with Christ, and He will give you the power you need to accomplish your purpose over the long haul. He will reignite your waning fire, allowing you to once more serve Him wholeheartedly.

4. Sadness

The disappointment, rage, bitterness, and animosity brought on by prior wrongs will not be vanquished by your goal. Betrayal, rejection, or abandonment can leave you with severe emotional wounds and a broken heart. Thus, it is a fallacy to think that discovering your mission will make you happy, cheerful, and enthusiastic. If you haven't dealt with your emotional baggage from before you found your purpose, it will still be there.

Don't evaluate your life's journey against that of others. Concentrate on your recovery process.

You may find yourself stuck and unable to let go of the hurt if you still harbor soul attachments to ex-partners, feel anguish for the person who injured you, or harbor resentment toward your father for his cruel words and deeds. Because *what if* holds you back, it is challenging to serve God when you have a damaged heart. What if he returned? What if I decide otherwise? What if I fail? What if I prefer a different option? You are weighed down with emotional baggage, which prevents you from achieving your life's mission.

God heals all wounds; time does not. Jesus came to release people who are captive to their emotions and to cure the brokenhearted. Wholeness recovery is a process that requires time. When you are entirely whole, you may truly love God with all of your heart, soul, and strength, and God will give you the ability to carry out His will.

5. Family Curses

Many purpose-searchers believe that if you discover your purpose, life will be easy, and you'll achieve the success you've always wanted. They encounter obstacles they can't see or get around, once they realize their goals and begin the effort.

You can toil for years with little advancement in your task unless God makes the barriers in your path clear to you. You will encounter many insurmountable obstacles along the way that are a result of your bloodline. Among many other things, generational curses can be seen in oppressive cycles, family patterns, recurrent failure, and persistent rejection.

Have you, for instance, started working at a job, but after a few months, your boss fired you for no reason of your own? Or, despite their talent, do your family members fail to prosper? Do others perpetually become engaged but never wed? According to Deuteronomy 28, there are numerous curses that come in a variety of forms and sizes.

God wants you to succeed in the work He has given you. Remember that Jesus has given you His authority to dismantle all of the enemy's power whenever you face the challenges that you have faced your entire life. Evaluate the areas of your life where you frequently experience failure or oppression in order to determine whether there are generational curses at work in your life. Ask God to reveal the curses that are keeping you from achieving your goals.

Remember that the five problems I've mentioned above are just the most frequent ones that prevent you from achieving your God-given assignment. Because everyone's life pathway is unique, there are many more.

You can choose the best course of action by understanding what is holding you back. God states that ignorance will cause us to perish. Don't let the enemy convince you to withdraw and stop serving God because he is keeping the true source of your problems a secret from you. God invites us to call upon Him with any questions we might have regarding our lives. He says,

> Call to me, and I will answer you, and tell you great and unsearchable things you do not know. (Jeremiah 33:3)

As you carry out the purpose that God has given you, heed the Holy Spirit's guidance. He will lead the way, and He will take away anything that stands in your path to the achievement He has in store for you.

Identifying Your Purpose Can Improve Life Quality

For your life to be meaningful, you must discover your purpose. The significance of discovering your purpose and how it might enhance your quality of life are as follow:

1. Finding Meaning in Life Requires a Purpose

Your mission, which can result in better relationships and physical health, is what motivates you to get out of bed each morning. Only 25 percent of American adults, according to a study, feel a distinct sense of purpose. Without a defined goal, life can become dull and unfulfilling. Your life will never be the same again, once you discover and comprehend your purpose.

You'll attract things into your life that you've always desired. You'll be prosperous, healthy, and at peace. Keep in mind that everything begins inside. Your external environment perfectly mirrors your internal environment. Fear, worry, and poverty will always be the by-products of a life without purpose. If you want to live a meaningful life, be aware of the way you think, and set aside some time each day to discover and clarify your purpose.

2. You'll Understand Yourself More Completely

Most of us believe that we are self-aware, but only a select handful have a deeper understanding of who they are. Gaining self-awareness will boost your self-esteem and enhance your quality of life. As you work toward your genuine purpose, you'll become aware of your exceptional qualities and hidden skills. You will identify your strengths and limitations during this procedure. You'll draw adventure and confidence into your life by embracing yourself as you are and making every effort to grow.

3. You'll Test Your Limiting Assumptions

Every purpose begins with a strong desire for a particular circumstance. In most situations, the person you aspire to be may not be living the life you are currently experiencing.

As a result, you might wonder if your mission can come to pass in your life, given the resources and abilities you currently lack. The reason that purpose is so potent is that you are positively challenged by it. Finding the required resources and honing your talents will be much easier. You can change your life by simply rephrasing your constricting beliefs. Remember that your exterior world reflects your inner world. You therefore must identify your purpose.

CONCLUSION

Women are endowed with the ability to give birth to future generations and to incubate destinies. This effect will last beyond the life of the individual woman only if she can stay by her purpose.

Finding your life's meaning can be a hard and overwhelming process. It can appear to be a vast, complicated, and frustrating subject. You want to advance, but you're unsure of how to do so. You're searching for your calling yet feel as though you're lost in the wilderness.

You may rely on God to guide you in the direction that He desires. He will take you alongside peaceful rivers; as Psalm 23:2–3 states,

> He makes me to lie down in green pastures; He leads me beside the still waters. He restores my soul; He leads me in the paths of righteousness For His name's sake.

God is not confused, but you could be.

Rise in strength is a rallying cry for God's women to realize their full potential as women of valor, fierce tenacity, bravery, and faith. In these hard times, God has endowed us with all the strength, power, and spiritual gifts we need to stay firm. God has given us the inner fortitude and faith necessary to face and overcome the difficulties of our day.

We need to accept God as our personal Lord and Savior as women. We must completely submit to God and wait on the Lord in confidence, putting our faith in Him to bolster and renew us. No matter how worn out we grow or how challenging our situations become, His grace is enough for us, and His might is made complete in our frailty.

Ruth is a wonderful example of a biblical lady who rose up in power. She was a heathen widow who, by virtue of her faith, turned out to be essential to God's plan for both the world's salvation and the future of Israel. The tragedy that befell Naomi and her two daughters-in-law in the land of Moab is the first real incident in the book of Ruth.

Ruth and Naomi learned about God's highest plan for them as a result of the hardships they endured. Ruth is the definition of fortitude, allegiance, diligence, and love. Her love for Naomi is unmatched. Ruth is self-motivated, as seen in Ruth 2:1. We should be self-motivated as women.

Those who are called by their destinies are self-motivated. Ruth would have continued worshiping alien deities, become a citizen of a cursed country, and remained forever outside of God's favor. She decided to become more powerful. She put forth a lot of effort—she was modest, she wasn't self-centered, and she had a servant's heart. Women, remember that!

God is telling all women to come up in power. Be a person of virtue, like Ruth. God wants us to strive toward this. God chose Ruth because she served as a role model for her virtues of graciousness, patience, and self-sacrifice.

Ruth teaches women who want to become stronger and find fulfillment in their lives. Consider the following points:

1. Your past is not a projection of your present or future. Don't give up! Ruth bravely forged ahead, following her mother-in-law, Naomi, and looked for a better future,

despite her predicament and history. She refused to let difficulties bring her down.

Your past shouldn't hold you back from moving forward and fulfilling your destiny. Move on with your purpose.

2. Have faith in God. Ruth, despite her youth, showed extraordinary faith. She had faith that God would take care of both her mother-in-law and her. Her belief in God and her trust in Him governed her life.
3. She learned that the God of Israel is impartial. Ruth belonged to the cursed Moabites. Only through marriage was she an Israelite. God loved her equally, despite that others viewed her as inferior. God is impartial.

Once you have faith and trust in God, nobody is unimportant in His eyes. His blessing is enough for everyone.

4. Character is important. Character is who you are when no one is looking.

Entreat me not to leave you, Or to turn back from following after you; For wherever you go, I will go; And wherever you lodge, I will lodge; Your people shall be my people, And your God, my God. (Ruth 1:16)

She probably never considered that, for centuries, millions would read about her and discover her character and selflessness. She significantly surpassed what was expected of a daughter-in-law. She treated Naomi with respect and was a good wife to Boaz, her second husband. She was a respectable woman whose attire reflected decorum, order, and dignity.

You desire to accomplish your destiny. You must be a selfless, honorable, and honest woman.

5. Everyone can find redemption. Ruth demonstrated by her faith and life that redemption is a gift from God and open to everyone, regardless of background.

   You will be redeemed, just as God redeemed Ruth.

6. Uphold your pledge with loyalty. Ruth kept her promise to Naomi. She stuck to her word, and God gave her a new husband and a new house as a reward.

What motivates you in life? Is it to be loved by the Lord? Which emotion governs your life more—guilt or anger? Is consumerism your driving force, or is it anger, fear, or resentment? Ruth led a life that had meaning.

Knowing your mission makes life easier. Knowing your mission helps you live intentionally and inspires you to overcome obstacles, like Ruth did.

> But they that wait upon the Lord shall renew their strength; they shall soar up with wings as eagles; they shall run and not be weary; and they shall walk and not be faint. (Isaiah 40:31)

Here, one is urged to wait on the Lord.

Women are encouraged to wait on the Lord if we want to grow stronger in our faith and fulfill His purpose for us. We need to give God our complete trust. Only then will we be able to run without ever losing our breath and walk without becoming tired. May we rise up in power, realizing our purpose and destiny!

The days of barely getting by and barely scraping the surface have passed, beloved. I proclaim that you will live a purposeful life. You will fulfill the divine assignment that God has planned for you. Nothing will shorten your life. Favor will watch over you today as you complete your task. Sit back, relax, and unwrap your special assignment for God's glory and your ultimate good.